D0530417

THE
COCKTAIL YEARS
365 Happy Hours

igloo

Published in 2006
by Igloo Books Ltd
Cottage Farm,
Sywell,
NN6 0BJ.
www.igloo-books.com

© Igloo Books Ltd 2006

All rights reserved. No part of this publication may be reproduced, stored
in a retrieval system, or transmitted in any way or by any means,
electronic, mechanical, photocopying, recording or otherwise, without the
prior written permission of the publisher.

10 9 8 7 6 5 4 3 2 1

ISBN: 1 84561 405 4

Project management: Metro Media Ltd

Author: Tina Lofthouse

Project coordinator: Adam Phillips
Layout artist: Tom Lynton
Cover image: Verner Panton
Cover design: Zoe Naylor
Photography: Anna Bond and FoodPix
Picture research: Jo St Mart

Thanks to: Cyrus Shahrad, Judy Keogh and
Vitra Design Museum/Verner Panton Design

Printed in China

Introduction

The cocktail – a boozy concoction to improve the performance of birds in cockfights (aka 'the cocks' ale')? A concoction named after a beautiful girl called Coctel, perhaps? Or the result of a toast made by soldiers in honor of a drink decorated with a feather? There are many stories said to be the 'true' origin of the cocktail and they are as much debated as the recipes for many of the cocktails themselves.

How do you make the ultimate dry martini, for example? The argument has become so extreme that some mixologists almost dispense with the dry vermouth altogether so you're basically drinking neat gin – albeit in a sophisticated glass.

So, if there is so much in dispute, why does a recipe matter? Because there are literally thousands of possible permutations for a mixed drink but only hundreds that are actually palatable. And from those hundreds, this book brings you 365 delicious recipes for every day of the year. But that's not all – there are also palette-pleasing recipes for special occasions too. Go on, indulge yourself!

Contents

The Measurements

Cocktails are given a bad name by those who tip the entire contents of their drinks cabinet into a pint glass, and chuck in some cream and whatever else is lurking in the fridge for good measure. In this book, we've used the standard for measuring cocktails – the US fluid ounce. This translates as 1 fl. oz. = 30 ml = 3 cl. Jiggers are often used to measure ingredients for cocktails but they can vary in size. A dash is a small amount of liquid – around 1/32 fl. oz. or about 1 ml. A cup is 8 fl. oz. or 236 ml.

The Alcohol

Cocktails are not an excuse to get rid of that dodgy liqueur you brought back from foreign climes five years ago – quality ingredients are a prerequisite for any decent cocktail. That is not to say you need Bombay Sapphire or Bollinger for every cocktail that calls for gin or champagne, but nor does it mean you should use the kind of bargain bucket liquor that, if swapped with paint stripper, you wouldn't notice the difference.

The Glasses

Glasses are important. A martini just wouldn't be the same served out of a highball glass – for one, you'd have to look hard to actually see the drink. There are a vast number of different glasses available but, unless you have plenty of money to burn on glasses you're only likely to use once a decade, you can get away with having just the following:

Rocks glass: Short, with thick bottom. It's also known as the lowball or old-fashioned glass.

Tall, straight highball glass: This can also be used instead of a Collins glass, although a Collins glass is slightly larger.

Champagne flute: An elegant glass for sparkling drinks; having a wine glass to hand is also recommended.

Cocktail glass: Also known as a martini glass, with its distinct sloping sides and graceful, long stem.

For those who want to spoil themselves, it would also be good to have a margarita glass, a heatproof glass with a handle, and a liqueur glass.

The Technique

There are a few techniques that are commonly referred to in cocktail-making that you need to know. To shake a cocktail requires a cocktail shaker three-quarters full of ice-cubes – add your ingredients and shake firmly until the outside of the shaker frosts. To stir with ice – add your ingredients to a mixing glass with ice cubes. Stir the ingredients gently but thoroughly. This chills the drink, imparting the right amount of water but without diluting it too much. Then you'll need a strainer to strain the drink into the glass. Oh, and make sure the glass is chilled too.

You may also need a blender for some recipes – use crushed ice rather than cubes. A long-handled bar spoon also comes in handy: one end has a muddler to crush herbs and fruit, the other end is useful as a measure and to layer ingredients in cocktails such as the Pousse-Café.

Simple syrup/sugar syrup is a vital ingredient in many cocktails. It can be made in advance and stored in the refrigerator. Combine one part water to one part sugar in a saucepan and boil for a couple of minutes. Recipes that call for a twist of lemon mean you should pare a strip of lemon – without the white pith – squeeze it over the drink to release the citrus oils and drop the twist into the drink.

And Finally..

Some of the recipes featured in this book include the use of raw eggs – please bear in mind that it is inadvisable for sick, elderly, or pregnant people to eat raw eggs.

1st **New Year's Day**

▶ Bloody Mary

1½ fl. oz. (45 ml) vodka   Tomato juice to fill
Dash Worcestershire sauce   Dash Tabasco sauce
Pinch of celery salt   Dash lemon juice

Mix the ingredients together over ice cubes in a highball glass.
Finish with a thin stick of celery.

Black Pearl

¼ fl. oz. (7 ml) cognac   ¼ fl. oz. (7 ml) Tia Maria
Champagne

Mix ingredients with ice in a mixing glass. Strain into a flute. Top
up with champagne and finish with a black cherry.

Sloe Driver

1½ fl. oz. (45 ml) sloe gin   Orange juice

Pour the gin over ice in a highball glass. Top up with orange juice,
stir, and finish with a slice of orange.

Cherry Rum Fizz

2 fl. oz. (60 ml) cherry brandy
Juice of ½ a lemon   Soda water

Shake brandy and lemon with ice and strain over ice cubes in a
highball glass. Top up with soda.

2nd **Resolution** (non-alcoholic)

Juice of a ½ a lemon   2 fl. oz. (60 ml) cranberry juice
2 tbsp honey   Hot water to fill

Add the ingredients to a heatproof glass or mug and mix well.

3rd **Hot Buttered Rum**

1¾ fl. oz. (52 ml) dark rum   1 tsp sugar
Hot water   Butter

Pour the rum, sugar, and water into a heatproof glass. Dot the
surface with butter and stir gently.

4th **Balmoral**

1½ fl. oz. (45 ml) Scotch whisky   ½ fl. oz. (15 ml) dry vermouth
½ fl. oz. (15 ml) sweet vermouth   Dash Angostura bitters

Stir the ingredients in a mixing glass half-filled with ice cubes.
Strain into a cocktail glass.

Bloody Mary

A spicy pick-me-up, perfect for cold days. The drinker
should be given the bottles of Tabasco and
Worcestershire sauce so they can add to taste!

5th   Casablanca

2 fl. oz. (60 ml) light rum $\frac{1}{2}$ fl. oz. (15 ml) fresh lime juice
$\frac{1}{4}$ fl. oz. (7 ml) orange curaçao $\frac{1}{4}$ fl. oz. (7 ml) cherry liqueur
Dash Angostura bitters

Shake ingredients together with ice cubes, then strain into a
cocktail glass.

6th ▶ Fallen Angel

$1\frac{1}{2}$ fl. oz. (45 ml) gin
1 fl. oz. (30 ml) fresh lemon juice
$\frac{1}{4}$ fl. oz. (7 ml) white crème de menthe
Dash Angostura bitters

Shake ingredients together with ice and strain into cocktail glass.

7th   Brandy Grog

$1\frac{1}{2}$ fl. oz. (45 ml) brandy   Sugar cube
Juice $\frac{1}{2}$ lemon   Hot water to top up

Dissolve sugar with some hot water in a heatproof glass. Add
brandy and lemon. Top up with hot water.

8th   Hot Cider Cup

Serves 6
6 cups cider $\frac{1}{4}$ cup brown sugar
$\frac{1}{2}$ lemon studded with 4 cloves   2 cinnamon sticks

Heat the ingredients gently in a saucepan, then strain into
heatproof glasses.

9th   Chocolate Martini

$1\frac{1}{2}$ fl. oz. (45 ml) vodka
1 fl. oz. (30 ml) white crème de cacao

Dip the rim of a cocktail glass in a saucer of cocoa powder. Shake
ingredients together with ice. Strain into a cocktail glass. Finish
with a chocolate-covered coffee bean.

10th   Whiskey Collins

$1\frac{1}{2}$ fl. oz. (45 ml) whiskey $\frac{1}{2}$ tsp sugar
1 fl. oz. (30 ml) fresh lemon juice   Soda water

Shake the ingredients together with ice. Strain into a Collins
glass or highball over ice. Top up with soda water.

11th   Detoxer (non-alcoholic)

2 tbsps mixed fresh berries   1 tsp sugar
Juice $\frac{1}{2}$ lime   Ginger ale

Muddle the berries with the sugar in a highball glass. Top up with
ginger ale and the juice of half a lime. Stir well and add ice.

Fallen Angel

This minty apéritif is traditionally made with white crème de menthe, but you can use green for a colorful cocktail.

12th ▶ Irish Coffee

1½ fl. oz. (45 ml) Irish whiskey
1 tsp brown sugar
Hot coffee to fill
Lightly whipped cream to serve

Stir together the ingredients in a heatproof glass or Irish Coffee glass. Float cream on the top.

13th Gimlet

1½ fl. oz. (45 ml) gin   ¾ fl. oz. (22 ml) Rose's lime juice

Shake ingredients with ice and strain into a cocktail glass. Finish with a twist of lime – the Rose's lime juice is essential for this simple cocktail.

14th Yellow Bird

1½ fl. oz. (45 ml) light rum   ½ fl. oz. (15 ml) Galliano
½ fl. oz. (15 ml) Cointreau
½ fl. oz. (15 ml) lemon juice

Shake ingredients with ice and strain into a cocktail glass.

15th Black Velvet

Stout   Champagne

Half-fill a champagne glass with stout, then top carefully with the champagne.

16th Sherry Flip

1½ fl. oz. (45 ml) sherry
¾ fl. oz. (22 ml) brandy
1 tsp sugar
½ fl. oz. (15 ml) cream
1 egg

Shake ingredients with ice and strain into a cocktail glass. Finish with a grating of nutmeg.

17th White Russian

1 fl. oz. (30 ml) vodka   ¾ fl. oz. (22 ml) coffee liqueur
2 tsp light cream

Pour vodka and liqueur over ice in a rocks glass. Float the cream on top.

18th English Rose

1 fl. oz. (30 ml) gin   ½ fl. oz. (15 ml) dry vermouth
½ fl. oz. (15 ml) apricot brandy   ½ fl. oz. (15 ml) lemon juice
1 tsp grenadine

Shake ingredients with ice and strain into a cocktail glass. Decorate with a maraschino cherry.

Irish Coffee

You can finish with whipped cream or use the back of a bar spoon to layer pouring cream on the top of the coffee.

19th　Chi Chi

1½ fl. oz. (45 ml) vodka　　　　2 fl. oz. (60 ml) coconut cream
2 fl. oz. (60 ml) pineapple juice

Combine ingredients with ice in a blender. Mix until smooth.
Serve in a hurricane glass or highball.

20th　Bentley

1 fl. oz. (30 ml) calvados　　　　1 fl. oz. (30 ml) Dubonnet

Mix ingredients with ice and strain into a cocktail glass.

21st　Corkscrew

½ fl. oz. (15 ml) white rum　　　½ fl. oz. (15 ml) dry vermouth
½ fl. oz. (15 ml) peach brandy

Shake the ingredients in a shaker with ice. Strain into a cocktail
glass. Finish with a slice of fresh lime.

22nd　Dry Martini

2 fl. oz. (60 ml) gin　　　　　　¼ fl. oz. (7 ml) dry vermouth

Stir ingredients with ice. Strain into a cocktail glass. Drop a green
olive into the drink.

23rd　Old-Fashioned

1½ fl. oz. (45 ml) bourbon　　　Dash Angostura bitters
2 tsp soda water　　　　　　　½ tsp sugar

Mix sugar, bitters, and water in an old-fashioned glass. Pour the
bourbon over it, add a few ice cubes and stir. Finish with half
slices of lemon, orange, and a maraschino cherry.

24th　Americano

1 fl. oz. (30 ml) Campari　　　　1 fl. oz. (30 ml) sweet red vermouth
Soda water

Add ingredients to a rocks glass over ice cubes. Stir and top up
with soda water. Finish with a twist of lemon.

25th　Burns Night

▶ The Robbie Burns (also known as the Bobbie Burns)

It is not known if this cocktail was named after the great Scot, or
named after someone known to the bar in which it was created!

1½ fl. oz. (45 ml) sweet vermouth
1½ fl. oz. (45 ml) Scotch whisky
3 dashes Benedictine

Shake ingredients with ice and strain into a cocktail glass.

The Robbie Burns

Scotch whisky is the essential ingredient for any Burns Supper. 'Whisky' comes from the Gaelic 'uisge beatha', meaning 'water of life'.

25th **Burns Night** (continued)

▶ ### Flying Scotsman

1¼ fl. oz. (37 ml) Scotch   1¼ fl. oz. (37 ml) sweet vermouth
Dash aromatic bitters   ¼ tsp simple syrup

Stir with ice and strain into a cocktail glass.

26th **Brandy Smash**

1½ fl. oz. (45 ml) brandy   4 mint sprigs
1 lump brown sugar

Muddle the mint and sugar with a little water in a rocks glass.
Add the brandy and ice.

27th **Manhattan**

1½ fl. oz. (45 ml) rye whiskey
¾ fl. oz. (22 ml) sweet vermouth
Dash Angostura bitters (optional)

Stir with ice and strain into a cocktail glass. Finish with a cherry.

28th **Italian Martini**

2 fl. oz. (60 ml) gin
¼ fl. oz. (7 ml) amaretto

Stir with ice and strain into a cocktail glass. Finish with a single
coffee bean.

29th **Chinese New Year**

(date varies from year to year)

Lychee Martini

1 fl. oz. (30 ml) vodka   1 fl. oz. (30 ml) lychee liqueur

Shake ingredients with ice. Strain into a cocktail glass and serve
with a peeled lychee.

30th **Acapulco**

1¼ fl. oz. (37 ml) light rum   ½ fl. oz. (15 ml) fresh lime juice
¼ fl. oz. (7 ml) Cointreau   ½ egg white
½ tsp sugar

Shake ingredients with ice and strain into a cocktail glass.

31st **Amaretto Sour**

1¼ fl. oz. (45 ml) amaretto   ¾ fl. oz. (22 ml) lemon juice
2 tsp sugar

Shake ingredients with ice and strain into a sours glass.

Flying Scotsman

When aromatic bitters are called for in a recipe, you can
choose between the main brands – Angostura,
Peychaud's, or Fee Brothers.

FEBRUARY

1st Brandy Sour

2 fl. oz. (60 ml) brandy   Juice of ½ lemon   ½ tsp sugar

Shake ingredients with ice and strain into a sours glass. Finish with a slice of lemon and a cherry.

2nd Groundhog Day

▶ The Groundhog

1½ fl. oz. (45 ml) dark rum   4 fl. oz. (120 ml) lime juice
¼ tsp sugar syrup   Ginger beer

Shake the rum and lime juice with ice. Strain into a highball glass over ice, and top up with ginger beer. Decorate with a lime wheel.

3rd Breakfast Martini

The ultimate hangover cure? This drink is sometimes served with a corner of toast!

1½ fl. oz. (45 ml) gin   ¾ fl. oz. (22 ml) triple sec
¾ fl. oz. (22 ml) freshly-squeezed lemon juice
1 tsp orange marmalade

Shake the ingredients together with ice. Strain into a cocktail glass.

4th Lemon Drop

1½ fl. oz. (45 ml) citrus vodka   ½ fl. oz. (15 ml) orange liqueur

Shake ingredients with ice and strain into a sugar-rimmed cocktail glass. Finish with a twist of lemon.

5th Negroni

¾ fl. oz. (22 ml) sweet vermouth   ¾ fl. oz. (22 ml) Campari
¾ fl. oz. (22 ml) gin

Pour ingredients over ice in a rocks glass. Stir. Finish with a slice of orange.

6th Planter's Punch

2 fl. oz. (60 ml) dark rum   2 fl. oz. (60 ml) pineapple juice
½ fl. oz. (15 ml) lemon juice   ½ fl. oz. (15 ml) grenadine
1 tsp sugar syrup

Mix all the ingredients in a highball glass with ice. Finish with a skewer of fruits.

7th Perfect Martini

1½ fl. oz. (45 ml) gin   ½ fl. oz. (15 ml) dry vermouth
½ fl. oz. (15 ml) sweet vermouth

Pour ingredients over ice in a mixing glass. Stir, then strain into a cocktail glass. Serve with a twist of lemon. Cocktails with 'Perfect' in the name have a balance of sweet and dry vermouth, rather than being 'perfect', although they may be!

The Groundhog

A classic mix of rum and ginger beer to celebrate (or commiserate) the news of whether or not spring is on its way.

8th **Red Lion**

¾ fl. oz. (22 ml) gin
¾ fl. oz. (22 ml) Grand Marnier
2 tsp orange juice
2 tsp lemon juice
Shake with ice and strain into a sugar-rimmed cocktail glass.

9th **Mai Tai**

1 fl. oz. (30 ml) light rum
1 fl. oz. (30 ml) dark rum
½ fl. oz. (15 ml) orange curaçao
½ fl. oz. (15 ml) orgeat syrup
¼ fl. oz. (7 ml) sugar syrup
Juice 1 fresh lime
Shake ingredients with ice and pour into a rocks glass over ice.
Decorate with a mint sprig and lime wedge.

10th **Sidecar**

¾ fl. oz. (22 ml) brandy   ¾ fl. oz. (22 ml) Cointreau
¾ fl. oz. (22 ml) lemon juice
Shake the ingredients with ice. Strain into a cocktail glass.

11th **Brooklyn**

1 fl. oz. (30 ml) whiskey
¾ fl. oz. (22 ml) red vermouth
¼ fl. oz. (7 ml) maraschino liqueur
Stir with ice and strain into a cocktail glass.

12th **Black Russian**

1½ fl. oz. (45 ml) vodka   1 fl. oz. (30 ml) coffee liqueur
Stir with ice. Strain into a rocks glass over ice.

13th **London Fog**

2 fl. oz. (60 ml) gin   ¼ fl. oz. (7 ml) licorice liqueur
Pour into a cocktail glass over ice.

14th **Valentine's Day**

▶ **Valentine**

Rosé champagne
Sugar lump
Dash Angostura bitters
Dash the bitters onto the sugar lump, place in a champagne flute
and top up with rosé champagne.

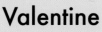

Valentine

Some chilled rosé champagne adds a touch of romance to the traditional champagne cocktail.

15th Frisco Sour

1½ fl. oz. (45 ml) bourbon
½ fl. oz. (15 ml) lemon juice
½ fl. oz. (15 ml) lime juice
½ fl. oz. (15 ml) Benedictine

Shake together with ice. Strain into a sours glass and finish with
a slice of lemon.

16th Virgin Mary (non-alcoholic)

4 fl. oz. (120 ml) tomato juice
Dash lemon juice
Dash Worcestershire sauce
Dash Tabasco sauce

Shake with ice and strain into a rocks glass over ice cubes.

17th Cuba Libra

1½ fl. oz. (45 ml) white rum
¼ fl. oz. (7 ml) fresh lime juice
Cola

Pour the rum and lime juice over ice in a highball glass. Top up
with cola. Finish with a wedge of lime.

18th Chocoholic

2 fl. oz. (60 ml) hazelnut liqueur
Hot chocolate made with milk to fill

Pour the liqueur and hot chocolate into a heatproof glass or mug.
Finish with whipped cream and a grating of rich, dark chocolate.

19th B&P

¾ fl. oz. (22 ml) brandy
¾ fl. oz. (22 ml) port

Stir the ingredients together in a rocks glass with ice.

20th Saketini

2 fl. oz. (60 ml) gin
½ fl. oz. (15 ml) sake

Stir with ice. Strain into a cocktail glass. Finish with a twist
of lemon.

21st ▶ Harvey Wallbanger

1 fl. oz. (30 ml) vodka
½ fl. oz. (15 ml) Galliano
Orange juice to fill

Pour vodka and orange juice over ice in a highball glass. Float
the Galliano on top. Finish with a slice of orange split over the
rim of the glass.

Harvey Wallbanger

Said to be named after a surfer who, after a few too many screwdrivers spiked with Galliano, kept bumping into the walls of the bar.

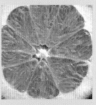

22nd Tequila Screwdriver

1½ fl. oz. (45 ml) tequila
Orange juice to fill

Mix with ice in a highball glass. Finish with an orange slice.

23rd Champagne Fizz

1½ fl. oz. (45 ml) gin
1 tsp sugar

1 fl. oz. (30 ml) lemon juice
Champagne

Shake ingredients with ice. Strain into a champagne flute. Top up
with champagne.

24th Daiquiri

1½ fl. oz. (45 ml) light rum
½ fl. oz. (15 ml) fresh lime juice
2 tsp sugar syrup

Shake all the ingredients with ice. Strain into a cocktail glass.

25th Moscow Mule

2 fl. oz. (60 ml) vodka
Ginger beer to fill

2 fl. oz. (60 ml) fresh lime juice

Mix in a highball glass with ice. Finish with a slice of lime.

26th New York

1½ fl. oz. (45 ml) bourbon
½ fl. oz. (15 ml) sugar syrup

2 dashes grenadine
¾ fl. oz. (22 ml) lemon juice

Shake ingredients with crushed ice. Strain into a cocktail glass.

27th Bailey's Coffee

2 fl. oz. (60 ml) Baileys Irish Cream
Hot, black coffee to fill

Pour ingredients into a heatproof glass, stir, and finish with
whipped cream and a sprinkling of cocoa.

28th Shrove Tuesday/ Pancake Day

(date varies from year to year)

▶ Royal Gin Fizz

2 fl. oz. (60 ml) gin
1 tsp sugar
Sparkling mineral water

Juice of ½ lemon
1 egg yolk

Shake ingredients with ice and strain into a highball glass over
ice. Top up with the sparkling water.

Royal Gin Fizz

This cocktail features some of the ingredients
traditionally used to make pancakes to celebrate Pancake
Day – eggs, lemon, and sugar!

MARCH

1st

St David's Day

Celebrate with the Welsh as they mark their patron saint's day. This cocktail is inspired by their national flag's emblem – the red dragon.

▶ The Dragon

³/₄ fl. oz. (22 ml) vodka   ³/₄ fl. oz. (22 ml) light rum
Cranberry juice to fill

Mix with ice in a rocks glass. Decorate with a wedge of lime.

Black Mountain Top

1 fl. oz. (30 ml) Black Mountain liqueur
Champagne

Add the liqueur to a champagne flute. Top up with champagne.
Finish with a couple of blackcurrants.

2nd

Gin Crusta

1¹/₂ fl. oz. (45 ml) gin   ¹/₂ fl. oz. (15 ml) lemon juice
¹/₂ fl. oz. (15 ml) triple sec   Dash orange bitters
¹/₄ fl. oz. (7 ml) maraschino liqueur

Run a lemon wedge around the edge of a cocktail glass and dip the rim in sugar. Peel a whole lemon so you are left with a spiral of peel that will fit inside the glass like a lining. Shake the other ingredients with ice and strain into the cocktail glass.

3rd

Pina Colada

1¹/₂ fl. oz. (45 ml) light rum   2 fl. oz. (60 ml) coconut milk
3 tbsp crushed pineapple

Mix the ingredients in a blender with ice. Serve in a highball glass with a straw.

4th

Between The Sheets

¹/₂ fl. oz. (15 ml) brandy   ¹/₂ fl. oz. (15 ml) triple sec
¹/₂ fl. oz. (15 ml) light rum   Juice of ¹/₄ lemon

Shake ingredients with ice and strain into a cocktail glass.

5th

Monte Carlo

1¹/₂ fl. oz. (45 ml) bourbon   ³/₄ fl. oz. (22 ml) Benedictine
Dash Angostura bitters

Stir with ice and strain into a cocktail glass.

6th

Bullshot

1¹/₂ fl. oz. (45 ml) vodka   3 fl. oz. (90 ml) beef consommé
Dash Tabasco

Mix ingredients with ice in a highball glass.

The Dragon

You can add half soda water and half cranberry juice for a hissing dragon variation.

7th Havana Hot Chocolate

1½ fl. oz. (45 ml) dark rum
3 tbsp dark chocolate powder
Hot milk
Whipped cream to decorate

Mix the chocolate powder with the rum in a heatproof glass. Top
up with hot milk, stir, and decorate with the whipped cream.

8th Godfather

1½ fl. oz. (45 ml) bourbon
½ fl. oz. (15 ml) amaretto

Pour ingredients over ice in a rocks glass. Finish with a quarter of lime.

9th Shirley Temple

1 fl. oz. (30 ml) grenadine
1 fl. oz. (30 ml) lime juice
Ginger ale to fill

Pour ingredients into an ice-filled highball glass. Finish with a
slice of orange and a cherry.

10th Scarlet O'Hara

1½ fl. oz. (45 ml) Southern Comfort
1¼ fl. oz. (37 ml) cranberry juice
¼ fl. oz. (7 ml) lime juice

Shake ingredients with ice. Strain into an ice-filled rocks glass.

11th Bermuda

2 fl. oz. (60 ml) gin
¾ fl. oz. (22 ml) peach brandy
1 fl. oz. (30 ml) orange juice
Dash blue curaçao

Shake ingredients with ice and strain into a cocktail glass. Finish
off with a slice of orange.

12th Blue Moon

1 fl. oz. (30 ml) blue curaçao
Champagne

Pour the curaçao into a champagne flute. Top up with champagne.

13th ▶ Red Wine Cooler

3 fl. oz. (90 ml) red wine
Dash grenadine
Soda water

Pour into a wine glass over ice. Top up with soda water.

BEAUJOLAI

APPELLATION BEAUJOLAIS
PRODUCE OF FRANCE

2005

SELECTED by TESCO
BOTTLED BY LOUIS JOSSE,
21700 NUITS-ST-GEORGES,
FRANCE.

12.5%vol   75cl

Red Wine Cooler

Some red wine cooler recipes use orange juice instead
of soda water. You can also add sugar to taste.

14th El Diablo

1¹/₂ fl. oz. (45 ml) tequila   ¹/₂ fl. oz. (15 ml) crème de cassis
¹/₂ fl. oz. (15 ml) fresh lime juice   Ginger ale

Pour ingredients over ice in a highball glass, then stir. Top up with
ginger ale and finish with a lime wedge.

15th Calvados Sour

1¹/₂ fl. oz. (45 ml) calvados   1 fl. oz. (30 ml) lemon
1 tsp sugar

Shake with ice and strain into a sours glass or cocktail glass.

16th Gin & It

1 fl. oz. (30 ml) gin   1 fl. oz. (30 ml) sweet red vermouth

Stir with ice and strain into a cocktail glass. Decorate with a
maraschino cherry on a cocktail stick.

17th St Patrick's Day

The patron saint of Ireland is celebrated on March 17th. Mark the
occasion with one of the many Guinness cocktails or try a classic
that uses Irish whiskey.

▶ Irish Rose

1¹/₂ fl. oz. (45 ml) Irish whiskey
³/₄ fl. oz. (22 ml) lemon juice
2 tsp grenadine

Shake ingredients with ice and strain into a cocktail glass.

Guinness Float

3 scoops ice cream
1 bottle of Guinness

Add ice cream to a highball glass. Top slowly with the Guinness.

Irish Fix

1¹/₂ fl. oz. (45 ml) Irish whiskey
¹/₂ fl. oz. (15 ml) Irish Mist
¹/₂ fl. oz. (15 ml) fresh lemon juice
¹/₂ tsp sugar syrup

Shake ingredients with ice and strain into an ice-filled
rocks glass.

St Patrick's Day

³/₄ fl. oz. (22 ml) green crème de menthe
³/₄ fl. oz. (22 ml) Irish whiskey
Dash Angostura bitters

Shake ingredients with ice and strain into a cocktail glass.

Irish Rose

Grenadine is a syrup made from pomegranates. Make your own by boiling pomegranate juice with an equal amount of sugar until it thickens slightly.

18th French Connection

1 fl. oz. (30 ml) cognac
³/₄ fl. oz. (22 ml) amaretto

Stir with ice in a rocks glass.

19th Chocatini

1¹/₄ fl. oz. (37 ml) vodka
¹/₄ fl. oz. (7 ml) Godiva liqueur

Shake vodka and liqueur with ice and strain into a cocktail glass.

20th Cola Float

2 fl. oz. (60 ml) bourbon
2 scoops ice cream
1 can cola

Place ice cream in a highball glass. Add bourbon, carefully top up with cola.

21st ▶ Pink Lady

1¹/₂ fl. oz. (45 ml) gin
1 egg white
1 tsp grenadine
1 tsp light cream

Shake ingredients with ice and strain into a cocktail glass.

22nd Ferrari

1 fl. oz. (30 ml) amaretto
1 fl. oz. (30 ml) dry vermouth

Stir with ice and strain into a cocktail glass. Serve up with a twist of lemon.

23rd Grasshopper

1 fl. oz. (30 ml) green crème de menthe
1 fl. oz. (30 ml) light cream
1 fl. oz. (30 ml) white crème de cacao

Shake over ice and strain into a cocktail glass.

24th Antifreeze

1¹/₂ fl. oz. (45 ml) dark rum
1 fl. oz. (30 ml) melon liqueur
1 fl. oz. (30 ml) pineapple juice

Shake ingredients with ice cubes, strain into a cocktail glass.

Pink Lady

Raw egg whites are used to give cocktails a frothy
texture. You can always buy pasteurized egg whites if
you prefer.

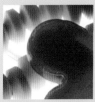

25th VLS

2 fl. oz. (60 ml) vodka
1 fl. oz. (30 ml) fresh lime juice
Soda water

Pour vodka into an ice-filled highball glass with the lime juice.
Top up with soda and finish with a slice of lime.

26th Brandy Sling

2 fl. oz. (60 ml) brandy
1 fl. oz. (30 ml) lemon juice
1 fl. oz. (30 ml) water
1 tsp sugar

Shake ingredients with ice and strain into a highball glass over ice.

27th Mimosa

2 fl. oz. (60 ml) orange juice   Champagne
1/2 fl. oz. (15 ml) orange curaçao

Add juice and curaçao to a champagne flute, then top up
with champagne.

28th ▶ Sweet Martini

1³/₄ fl. oz. (52 ml) gin
³/₄ fl. oz. (22 ml) sweet vermouth

Stir with ice. Strain into a cocktail glass.

29th Mexican Colada

1¹/₂ fl. oz. (45 ml) tequila
1 fl. oz. (30 ml) Kahlua
2 fl. oz. (60 ml) pineapple juice
¹/₄ fl. oz. (7 ml) coconut cream
³/₄ fl. oz. (22 ml) cream

Shake ingredients with ice. Strain into a highball glass over ice.

30th El Presidente

2 fl. oz. (60 ml) light rum
1 fl. oz. (30 ml) pineapple juice
1/2 fl. oz. (15 ml) lime juice
Dash grenadine

Shake ingredients with ice and strain into a cocktail glass.

31st Caipirinha

2 oz (60 ml) cachaça
1 lime cut into wedges
2 tsp sugar

In a rocks glass, muddle the lime wedges with the sugar. Add the
cachaça, top up with crushed ice and stir well.

Sweet Martini

Some say the 'godfather' of the martini is the Martinez, which calls for more sweet vermouth to gin. Today, how you mix is down to personal taste.

APRIL

1st — April Fool's Day

▶ The Joker

¾ fl. oz. (22 ml) light rum   ¾ fl. oz. (22 ml) cherry liqueur
Cola

Pour ingredients into an ice-filled rocks glass. Top up with cola.

Black Magic

1 fl. oz. (30 ml) vodka   1 fl. oz. (30 ml) coffee liqueur
Dash lemon juice

Pour ingredients over ice in a rocks glass. Stir and finish with a lemon slice.

Trickster

½ fl. oz. (15 ml) triple sec   ½ fl. oz. (15 ml) cherry brandy
Cava

Shake the triple sec and brandy with ice. Strain into a champagne flute and top up with cava.

2nd — Alexander

1 fl. oz. (30 ml) brandy   ¾ fl. oz. (22 ml) crème de cacao
¾ fl. oz. (22 ml) cream

Shake ingredients with ice and strain into a cocktail glass. Finish with a sprinkling of nutmeg.

3rd — Grapefruit Refresher (non-alcoholic)

¾ fl. oz. (22 ml) non-alcoholic grenadine
2 fl. oz. (60 ml) grapefruit juice
1 fl. oz. (30 ml) sugar syrup   Soda water

Shake ingredients with ice and strain into an ice-filled highball glass. Top up with soda water.

4th — Amaretto Coffee

2 fl. oz. (60 ml) amaretto   1 cup hot, black coffee
Whipped cream

Pour amaretto into a heatproof glass or mug. Add the coffee and top with whipped cream.

5th — Spring Fever

1½ fl. oz. (45 ml) gin   ½ fl. oz. (15 ml) green curaçao
Apple juice   Soda water

Pour gin and green curaçao into a highball glass over ice. Stir and top up with apple juice and soda.

The Joker

There's rum and cola and cherry liqueur – this all combines to bring the best of both worlds together in one fantastic cocktail.

6th Raspberry Crush

2 fl. oz. (60 ml) vodka
6 raspberries
1 tsp sugar

Shake ingredients with ice and strain into a cocktail glass. Finish with a single raspberry.

7th Kentucky Cocktail

1½ fl. oz. (45 ml) bourbon
¾ fl. oz. (22 ml) Benedictine

Stir with ice and strain into a cocktail glass.

8th Caipirissima

2 fl. oz. (60 ml) white rum
4 lime wedges
2 tbsp sugar

Muddle the lime wedges with the sugar in a rocks glass. Add the rum and fill with crushed ice.

9th Pear Champagne

1 tsp eau-de-vie Poire William
Champagne to fill

Add ingredients to champagne flute. Garnish with a slice of pear.

10th Gin & Tonic

2 fl. oz. (60 ml) gin
Wedge of lime
Tonic to fill

Pour the gin and tonic into an ice-filled highball glass. Squeeze the lime juice over the drink. Garnish with a slice of lime.

11th ▶ Brandy Cocktail

2 fl. oz. (60 ml) brandy
¼ tsp sugar syrup
Dash Angostura bitters

Stir with ice and strain into a cocktail glass. Finish with a twist of lemon.

12th Rum Martini

2 fl. oz. (60 ml) light rum
½ fl. oz. (15 ml) dry vermouth

Mix the ingredients in a mixing glass with ice. Strain into a cocktail glass.

Brandy Cocktail

Angostura bitters is an essential ingredient in many
cocktails. It was originally developed from a range of
herbs in 1824 as a medicine.

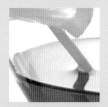

13th — White Spider

1 fl. oz. (30 ml) white crème de menthe
1 fl. oz. (30 ml) vodka

Pour ingredients over ice in a rocks glass.

14th — Black Devil

2 fl. oz. (60 ml) light rum $^1/_2$ fl. oz. (15 ml) dry vermouth

Stir with ice and strain into a cocktail glass. Serve with a
black olive.

15th — The Bramble

$1^1/_2$ fl. oz. (45 ml) gin
$^3/_4$ fl. oz. (22 ml) crème de mure
$^3/_4$ fl. oz. (22 ml) simple syrup
$^3/_4$ fresh lime juice

Shake all the ingredients, except the crème de mure, with ice.
Pour into an ice-filled rocks glass and pour the crème de mure
over the top but don't stir. Finish with fresh blackberries and a
sprig of mint.

16th — Orange & Pineapple Flip

(non-alcoholic)

2 fl. oz. (60 ml) orange juice   2 fl. oz. (60 ml) pineapple juice
$^3/_4$ fl. oz. (22 ml) lemon juice   1 egg yolk

Shake ingredients with ice and strain into an ice-filled
highball glass.

17th — Malibu Hot Chocolate

1 fl. oz. (30 ml) Malibu   Hot chocolate made with milk
Whipped cream

Add Malibu to mug, top up with hot chocolate and then decorate
with cream.

18th ▶ Pick Me Up

1 fl. oz. (30 ml) cognac   1 fl. oz. (30 ml) orange juice
Champagne

Stir the cognac and orange juice in a champagne flute. Top up
with chilled champagne.

19th — Lemongrass Martini

2 fl. oz. (60 ml) gin   1 stem lemongrass (sliced)
1 piece crystalized ginger

Muddle lemongrass with the ginger. Shake with the gin and ice
and strain into a cocktail glass. Finish with a thin, long sliver
of lemongrass.

Pick Me Up

With any cocktail that calls for champagne, make sure that the bottle is well-chilled before you begin mixing your drink.

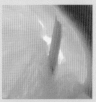

20th Pomegranate Cooler (non-alcoholic)

2 fl. oz. (60 ml) pomegranate juice
1/2 fl. oz. (15 ml) lime juice
1/2 tsp sugar
Soda water

Dissolve the sugar in the lime in a highball glass. Add ice. Add the juice and top up with soda.

21st Rose Petal Martini

1 1/2 fl. oz. (45 ml) vodka   Dash rose water
1/4 tsp sugar syrup   1/4 tsp lemon juice

Shake ingredients with ice and strain into a cocktail glass. Decorate with an edible rose petal.

22nd Cherry Flip

1 1/2 fl. oz. (45 ml) cherry brandy   1 egg
1 tsp sugar   1/2 fl. oz. (15 ml) cream

Shake ingredients with ice and strain into a cocktail glass. Finish with a sprinkling of nutmeg.

23rd St George's Day

England celebrates its patron saint. A red cocktail to match the red cross of the flag!

▶ St George

2 fl. oz. (60 ml) gin   1 fl. oz. (30 ml) fresh lime juice
Cranberry juice to fill

Pour ingredients into a highball glass over ice. Stir.

English Cobbler

2 fl. oz. (60 ml) Jamaican rum   1 fl. oz. (30 ml) tea
1 tsp sugar   1 tsp lemon juice

Shake with ice and strain into an ice-filled rocks glass.

English Mule

2 fl. oz. (60 ml) ginger wine   1 fl. oz. (30 ml) gin
2 fl. oz. (60 ml) orange juice   Soda water

Run a chunk of fresh ginger around the rim of a highball glass. Add ice, ginger wine, gin, and orange. Stir and top up with soda.

English Coffee

1 fl. oz. (30 ml) gin   1/2 fl. oz. (15 ml) coffee liqueur
Hot, strong, black coffee

Add gin and coffee liqueur to a heatproof glass. Top up with coffee. Sweeten to taste.

St George

Gin was originally a Dutch drink, but its long and illustrious association with the English started when soldiers were given gin – 'Dutch Courage' – during the Thirty Years War.

24th Dog's Nose

1 fl. oz. (30 ml) gin   Warmed ale

Add gin to a beer glass. Top up with ale.

25th South Coast

1¼ fl. oz. (37 ml) Scotch whisky
¼ fl. oz. (7 ml) orange liqueur
¼ fl. oz. (7 ml) fresh lemon
1 tsp sugar syrup
Dash orange juice

Stir ingredients in a mixing glass with ice. Strain into a cocktail
glass and top up with soda water.

26th Bay Breeze

1½ fl. oz. (45 ml) vodka   3 fl. oz. (90 ml) pineapple juice
Dash cranberry juice

Pour ingredients into a highball glass over ice.

27th Apple Turnover

1 fl. oz. (30 ml) apple brandy   Dash grenadine
Champagne

Pour ingredients into a champagne flute and then top up with
chilled champagne.

28th Prairie Oyster (non-alcoholic)

2 tbsp tomato catsup
Dash hot pepper sauce
3 dashes Worcestershire sauce
Freshly ground black pepper
1 egg yolk

Shake all the ingredients except the egg with ice. Strain into a
rocks glass. Add the egg yolk, taking care not to break it.

29th ▶ Pineapple Margarita

1½ fl. oz. (45 ml) tequila
¾ fl. oz. (22 ml) triple sec
½ fl. oz. (15 ml) fresh lime juice
3 pineapple rings

Place ingredients into a blender with ice. Blend and serve in a
salt-rimmed margarita glass.

30th Campari & Soda

2 fl. oz. (60 ml) Campari   Soda
Wedge of orange

Pour Campari into an ice-filled rocks glass. Top up with soda
water. Squeeze the juice from the orange wedge over the top.

Pineapple Margarita

Most varieties of fruit can be used when making the intoxicating frozen margarita cocktail. Try a mix of ripe mango and strawberry.

MAY

1st	**May Day**	Your Own Special Occasions and Cocktail Ratings

▶ May Day Cocktail

2 fl. oz. (60 ml) gin   1 fl. oz. (30 ml) lemon juice
1 fl. oz. (30 ml) sugar syrup   6 mint leaves

Muddle the mint, sugar, and lemon in a highball glass. Add the gin and top up with crushed ice. Finish with a sprig of mint.

2nd Alabama Slammer

$^1/_2$ fl. oz. (15 ml) Southern Comfort $^1/_2$ fl. oz. (15 ml) sloe gin
$^1/_2$ fl. oz. (15 ml) amaretto   Dash orange juice

Shake ingredients with ice and strain into a rocks glass over ice.

3rd Lime Daiquiri

$1^1/_4$ fl. oz. (37 ml) rum $1^1/_2$ fl. oz. (45 ml) lime juice
$1^1/_2$ fl. oz. (45 ml) sugar syrup

Shake ingredients with ice and strain into a cocktail glass. Finish with a twist of lime.

4th Cosmo Twist

$1^1/_2$ fl. oz. (45 ml) blackcurrant vodka
$^1/_4$ fl. oz. (7 ml) Cointreau   1 fl. oz. (30 ml) cranberry juice
$^1/_4$ fl. oz. (7 ml) fresh lime juice

Shake ingredients with ice and strain into a cocktail glass. Garnish with a couple of blackcurrants.

5th Pomegranate Margarita

$1^1/_2$ fl. oz. (45 ml) tequila   1 fl. oz. (30 ml) pomegranate juice
$^1/_2$ fl. oz. (15 ml) triple sec $^1/_2$ fl. oz. (15 ml) lime juice

Shake ingredients with ice and strain into a salt-rimmed margarita glass.

6th Mint Bite

1 fl. oz. (30 ml) cream $^1/_2$ fl. oz. (15 ml) crème de cacao
$^1/_2$ fl. oz. (15 ml) peppermint schnapps

Shake ingredients with ice and strain into a cocktail glass.

7th Jamaican Coffee

$1^1/_4$ fl. oz. (37 ml) Tia Maria   1 tsp sugar
Hot coffee to fill   Whipped cream

Add the ingredients to an Irish Coffee glass or mug. Finish with the cream.

May Day Cocktail

Whether you celebrate May Day as International Workers' Day or a pagan holiday, the combination of gin and mint makes for a lively cocktail.

8th

Isle of Skye

³/₄ fl. oz. (22 ml) gin   ³/₄ fl. oz. (22 ml) Drambuie
³/₄ fl. oz. (22 ml) lemon juice

Shake ingredients with ice and strain into a cocktail glass.

9th

Port Sangaree

2¹/₂ fl. oz. (75 ml) port
2 fl. oz. (60 ml) soda water
¹/₂ tsp sugar

Stir the port with the sugar in a highball glass. Add ice and soda.
Finish with a grating of nutmeg.

10th

Lady Godiva

1¹/₂ fl. oz. (45 ml) brandy
1 tsp sugar
2 dashes triple sec
¹/₄ fl. oz. (7 ml) lemon juice
¹/₄ fl. oz. (7 ml) lime juice

Shake all ingredients, except the brandy, with ice. Strain into a
highball glass and top up with the brandy.

11th

Lemon Martini

1 fl. oz. (30 ml) limoncello
1 fl. oz. (30 ml) vodka

Shake ingredients with ice and strain into a cocktail glass.

12th

Depth Charge

1 fl. oz. (30 ml) tequila   Glass of lager

Pour the tequila into a shot glass, then drop into the lager. Drink!

13th

Dirty Martini

2 fl. oz. (60 ml) gin
¹/₂ fl. oz. (15 ml) dry vermouth
Olive brine to taste
Olive to garnish

Stir the ingredients with ice in a mixing glass. Strain into a
cocktail glass. Finish with an olive.

14th **Mother's Day** (USA, date varies from year to year)

▶ Angel Face

1 fl. oz. (30 ml) gin
³/₄ fl. oz. (22 ml) apricot brandy
³/₄ fl. oz. (22 ml) apple brandy

Stir with ice and strain into a cocktail glass.

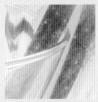

Angel Face

This classic drink uses two types of brandy, giving it a
wonderful fruity flavor. Gin gives it an extra kick.

14th Mother's Day (continued)

▶ Jaded Lady

¹/₂ fl. oz. (15 ml) gin
¹/₂ fl. oz. (15 ml) blue curaçao
¹/₂ fl. oz. (15 ml) advocaat
1 fl. oz. (30 ml) orange juice

Shake ingredients with ice and strain into a cocktail glass.

Bahama Mama

¹/₂ fl. oz. (15 ml) dark rum
¹/₄ fl. oz. (7 ml) coffee liqueur
¹/₄ fl. oz. (7 ml) coconut liqueur
¹/₄ fl. oz. (7 ml) 151 proof rum
4 fl. oz. (120 ml) pineapple juice
Juice of ¹/₂ lemon

Shake ingredients with ice and strain into an ice-filled
highball glass.

Celebration

1¹/₂ fl. oz. (45 ml) brandy   ¹/₄ fl. oz. (7 ml) sweet vermouth
¹/₄ fl. oz. (7 ml) dry vermouth   Dash orange juice

Stir ingredients with ice and strain into a cocktail glass. Finish
with an orange wheel.

Perfect Lady

1 fl. oz. (30 ml) gin
¹/₂ fl. oz. (15 ml) peach brandy
¹/₂ fl. oz. (15 ml) lemon juice
Dash egg white

Shake ingredients with ice and strain into a cocktail glass.

15th Robson

1¹/₂ fl. oz. (45 ml) light rum   ¹/₂ fl. oz. (15 ml) grenadine
¹/₂ fl. oz. (15 ml) orange juice   ¹/₂ fl. oz. (15 ml) lemon juice

Shake ingredients with ice and strain into a cocktail glass.

16th Yellow Jersey

3 fl. oz. (90 ml) Martini Rosso   Ginger ale

Pour ingredients over ice in a lowball glass. Fill with ginger ale.

17th Madras

2 fl. oz. (60 ml) vodka   2 fl. oz. (60 ml) cranberry juice
2 fl. oz. (60 ml) orange juice

Mix ingredients with ice in a highball glass.

Jaded Lady

For any mother in need of a pick-me-up! Check out the
fantastic color that results from the blue curaçao and
advocaat.

18th — Apple Brandy Rickey

1½ fl. oz. (45 ml) apple brandy
Juice ½ lime　　　　　　　　Soda water

Stir ingredients in a highball glass over ice. Top up with soda water.

19th ▶ Velvet Hammer

¾ fl. oz. (22 ml) crème de cacao
¾ fl. oz. (22 ml) vodka　　　　2 fl. oz. (60 ml) cream

Shake ingredients with ice and strain into a cocktail glass.

20th — Zombie

1½ fl. oz. (45 ml) lemon juice
¾ fl. oz. (22 ml) orange juice
¾ fl. oz. (22 ml) light rum
¾ fl. oz. (22 ml) dark rum
½ fl. oz. (15 ml) apricot brandy
½ fl. oz. (15 ml) pineapple juice
½ fl. oz. (15 ml) 151 proof rum

Shake everything, except the 151 proof rum, together with
ice. Strain into an ice-filled highball glass. Pour the 151 proof
rum over the top.

21st — Missouri Mule

1½ fl. oz. (45 ml) bourbon
¼ fl. oz. (7 ml) crème de cassis
¼ fl. oz. (7 ml) lemon juice

Shake ingredients with ice and strain into a cocktail glass.

22nd — Gin Daisy

1½ fl. oz. (45 ml) gin　　　　1 fl. oz. (30 ml) lemon juice
½ fl. oz. (15 ml) grenadine　　1 tsp sugar

Shake ingredients with ice and strain into a cocktail glass.

23rd — White Wine Cooler

5 fl. oz. (150 ml) chilled white wine
½ fl. oz. (15 ml) brandy
½ fl. oz. (15 ml) fresh lemon
Dash orange bitters　　　　　2 tsp sugar
1 tsp kummel　　　　　　　　Soda water

Pour ingredients into a highball glass over ice and top up with soda.

24th — Gingenstein

1 fl. oz. (30 ml) vodka　　　　½ fl. oz. (15 ml) red vermouth
1 tsp sugar syrup　　　　　　Ginger beer

Shake vodka, sugar syrup, and vermouth with ice. Strain into a
highball glass over ice. Top up with ginger beer.

Velvet Hammer

Crème de cacao gives cocktails a wonderful chocolate and vanilla flavor. It is available in brown or white (clear) – either can be used here.

25th ▶ Fifty Fifty Vodka Martini

1¼ fl. oz. (37 ml) vodka
1¼ fl. oz. (37 ml) dry vermouth

Stir with ice. Strain into a cocktail glass. Garnish with an olive.

26th Flying Dutchman

2 fl. oz. (60 ml) gin
½ fl. oz. (15 ml) orange liqueur

Stir ingredients with ice and strain into a cocktail glass.

27th Bloody Maria

2 fl. oz. (60 ml) tequila
Dash lemon juice
Tomato juice to fill
Worcestershire sauce
Tabasco sauce

Pour ingredients over ice in a highball glass. Stir.

28th Fluffy Duck

1 fl. oz. (30 ml) white rum
1 fl. oz. (30 ml) advocaat
Lemonade

Mix rum and advocaat in a highball glass with crushed ice. Top up
with lemonade. Finish with a strawberry.

29th Mississippi Mud

1½ fl. oz. (45 ml) Southern Comfort
1½ fl. oz. (45 ml) Kahlua
2 scoops vanilla ice cream

Blend ingredients with ice. Serve in a highball glass.

30th B&B

½ fl. oz. (15 ml) Benedictine
½ fl. oz. (15 ml) brandy

Pour Benedictine into a liqueur glass and then carefully float the
brandy on top.

31st Silver Bronx

1 fl. oz. (30 ml) gin
½ fl. oz. (15 ml) dry vermouth
½ fl. oz. (15 ml) sweet vermouth
¾ fl. oz. (22 ml) fresh orange juice
1 egg white

Shake ingredients with ice and strain into a cocktail glass.

Fifty Fifty Vodka Martini

Never leave your ice for too long before you mix your cocktail, or the end result will taste far too watery.

JUNE

1st — Alexander's Sister

Your Own Special Occasions and Cocktail Ratings

³/₄ fl. oz. (22 ml) gin
³/₄ fl. oz. (22 ml) green crème de menthe
³/₄ fl. oz. (22 ml) light cream

Shake ingredients with ice and strain into a cocktail glass.

2nd — Vodka Daisy

2 fl. oz. (60 ml) vodka
Juice of ¹/₂ lemon
¹/₂ tsp sugar
1 tsp grenadine

Shake ingredients with ice and strain into a lowball glass over ice.

3rd — Apple Blossom

1 fl. oz. (30 ml) calvados
¹/₄ fl. oz. (7 ml) grenadine
Lemonade

Mix calvados and grenadine in a highball glass with ice. Add lemonade to taste.

4th — Muddy River

1¹/₂ fl. oz. (45 ml) Kahlua
1 fl. oz. (30 ml) crème de cacao
1¹/₂ fl. oz. (45 ml) light cream

Mix ingredients together with ice in a rocks glass.

5th — Nutty Colada

2 fl. oz. (60 ml) amaretto
1¹/₂ fl. oz. (45 ml) coconut milk
3 pineapple chunks

Blend ingredients with ice until smooth. Serve in a highball glass.

6th — Salty Dog

1¹/₂ fl. oz. (45 ml) gin
3 fl. oz. (90 ml) grapefruit juice

Salt the rim of a highball glass. Shake the ingredients with ice. Strain into the highball glass over ice.

7th — ▶ Sundowner

2 fl. oz. (60 ml) vodka   2 fl. oz. (60 ml) orange
Dash sweet red vermouth

Shake with ice. Strain into a cocktail glass with a twist of lemon.

Sundowner

There are many variations on the vodka-and-orange
theme. The vermouth here lends depth to the drink.

8th Park Avenue Martini

1½ fl. oz. (45 ml) gin
¼ fl. oz. (7 ml) sweet vermouth
1 fl. oz. (30 ml) pineapple juice

Shake ingredients with ice and strain into a cocktail glass.

9th Brandy Cassis

1½ fl. oz. (45 ml) brandy
½ fl. oz. (15 ml) crème de cassis
1 fl. oz. (30 ml) fresh lemon juice

Shake ingredients with ice. Strain into a cocktail glass. Serve with a twist of lemon.

10th Whiskey Cooler

2 fl. oz. (60 ml) whiskey
1 tsp sugar syrup
1 fl. oz. (30 ml) fresh lime juice
Ginger beer

Shake the whiskey, fresh lime juice, and sugar syrup with ice. Strain into a highball glass over ice. Top up with ginger beer.

11th Journalist

1 fl. oz. (30 ml) gin
½ fl. oz. (15 ml) dry vermouth
½ fl. oz. (15 ml) sweet red vermouth
1 tsp lemon juice
Dash triple sec
Dash Angostura bitters

Shake ingredients with ice and strain into a cocktail glass.

12th ▶ Sherry Flip

1½ fl. oz. (45 ml) sherry
1 egg
½ fl. oz. (15 ml) cream
¼ fl. oz. (7 ml) brandy
1 tsp sugar

Shake ingredients with ice and strain into a cocktail glass.

13th Godmother

1 fl. oz. (30 ml) vodka
1 fl. oz. (30 ml) amaretto

Pour ingredients over ice in an old-fashioned glass. Stir.

14th Jamaican Fizz

2 fl. oz. (60 ml) dark rum
1½ fl. oz. (45 ml) pineapple juice
1 tsp sugar
Soda water

Shake all the ingredients, apart from the soda, with ice and strain into a highball glass over ice. Top up with soda water.

Sherry Flip

Flips use eggs and sometimes cream for a rich cocktail.
Sherry and brandy are the most popular – this recipe
uses both.

15th Hemingway Daiquiri

1 fl. oz. (30 ml) white rum
¼ fl. oz. (7 ml) maraschino liqueur
½ fl. oz. (15 ml) grapefruit juice
¾ fl. oz. (22 ml) fresh lime juice
Shake ingredients with ice and strain into a cocktail glass.

16th Napoleon

2 fl. oz. (60 ml) gin   ½ fl. oz. (15 ml) orange curaçao
½ fl. oz. (15 ml) Dubonnet
Stir ingredients with ice and strain into a cocktail glass.

17th **Father's Day** (UK only. Date varies from year to year)

▶ Rolls Royce

1 fl. oz. (30 ml) brandy   ¾ fl. oz. (22 ml) orange liqueur
¾ fl. oz. (22 ml) orange juice
Shake ingredients with ice and strain into a cocktail glass.

Million Dollar

1 fl. oz. (30 ml) gin   1 fl. oz. (30 ml) sweet vermouth
¼ fl. oz. (7 ml) grenadine   ¼ fl. oz. (7 ml) pineapple juice
1 tsp egg white
Shake ingredients with ice and strain into a cocktail glass.

Diplomat

1½ fl. oz. (45 ml) dry vermouth
½ fl. oz. (15 ml) sweet vermouth
1 tsp maraschino liqueur
Dash aromatic bitters
Shake ingredients with ice and strain into a cocktail glass. Finish
with a cherry on the rim.

Whiskey Sangaree

2 fl. oz. (60ml) whiskey   2 fl. oz. (60ml) soda water
1 tsp sugar   ½ fl. oz. (15 ml) port
Pinch nutmeg
Dissolve the sugar with a dash of water in a rocks glass. Add
ice, whiskey, and soda. Stir. Float the port on top and then finish
with nutmeg.

Black & Tan

½ glass ale   ½ glass stout
Pour the ale into a highball glass then use the back of a spoon to
float the stout on top.

Rolls Royce

For the father who likes the finer things in life. The touch
of orange liqueur works well with the brandy.

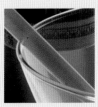

17th Father's Day (continued)

Country Gentleman

1 fl. oz. (30 ml) apple brandy
³/₄ fl. oz. (22 ml) orange curaçao
¹/₂ fl. oz. (15 ml) lemon juice
1 tsp sugar syrup

Shake ingredients with ice. Strain into a cocktail glass and finish
with a twist of lemon.

18th Gin Sour

2 fl. oz. (60 ml) gin   1 fl. oz. (30 ml) lemon juice
¹/₂ tsp sugar

Shake ingredients with ice and strain into a sours glass.

19th ▶ Hurricane

2 fl. oz. (60 ml) amber rum   2 fl. oz. (60 ml) passion-fruit juice
1 tsp sugar   ¹/₂ tsp grenadine
Juice ¹/₂ lime

Stir sugar with rum and passion-fruit juice until dissolved. Add all
the ingredients to a shaker with ice. Shake and strain into a
hurricane glass.

20th Floater

1 fl. oz. (30 ml) Scotch whisky   Soda water

Pour a little soda water into a highball glass, then slowly layer
the Scotch over the soda water.

21st Summer Solstice

1 fl. oz. (30 ml) vodka   ³/₄ fl. oz. (22 ml) cherry brandy
1 fl. oz. (30 ml) orange juice

Shake ingredients with ice and strain into a cocktail glass.

22nd Tinto De Verano (Red Wine Of Summer)

5 fl. oz. (150 ml) red wine   Lemonade

Fill a highball glass with ice. Pour in the red wine. Top up with
lemonade and garnish with a slice of lemon and slice of lime.

23rd Very Berry

1¹/₂ fl. oz. (45 ml) gin   ¹/₂ fl. oz. (15 ml) crème de cassis
2 tbsp mixed berries   1 tsp sugar

Muddle the sugar and berries. Shake all the ingredients with ice.
Strain into a cocktail glass.

Hurricane

The Hurricane was invented at Pat O'Brien's, a New Orleans bar. It should be served in a glass shaped like a hurricane lamp.

24th Chelsea Hotel

1½ fl. oz. (45 ml) gin
½ fl. oz. (15 ml) triple sec
1 fl. oz. (30 ml) lemon juice

Shake ingredients with ice and strain into a cocktail glass.

25th Woo Woo

2 fl. oz. (60 ml) vodka
½ fl. oz. (15 ml) peach schnapps
½ fl. oz. (15 ml) cranberry juice

Mix ingredients in a highball glass with ice.

26th Pimm's No 1

1½ fl. oz. (45 ml) Pimm's No 1
Lemonade
1 slice cucumber, orange, and lemon

Pour Pimm's over ice in a highball glass. Top up with lemonade.
Stir. Finish with cucumber, orange, and lemon.

27th Bourbon Daisy

2 fl. oz. (60 ml) bourbon
1 fl. oz. (30 ml) lemon juice
½ tsp grenadine
½ tsp sugar

Shake ingredients with ice and strain into a rocks glass over ice.

28th Rumless Rickey

1 fl. oz. (30 ml) lime juice
Dash grenadine
1 fl. oz. (30 ml) sugar syrup
Soda water

Pour ingredients over ice in an old-fashioned glass, then stir and
top up with soda water.

29th ▶ Cognac & Mint Frappé

1 fl. oz. (30 ml) cognac
¾ fl. oz. (22 ml) white crème de menthe

Build ingredients over crushed ice in a champagne flute.

30th Pink Gin

1½ fl. oz. (45 ml) gin
2 dashes Angostura bitters

Swirl the bitters around the cocktail glass, then add the gin.

Cognac & Mint Frappé

Frappés are drinks served over a glass of crushed ice. This minty version is a perfect drink for warm summer evenings.

JULY

1st	**Canada Day**	Your Own Special Occasions and Cocktail Ratings

▶ Canadian

1½ fl. oz. (45 ml) Canadian whisky   ½ fl. oz. (15 ml) triple sec
½ tsp sugar   Dash orange bitters

Shake ingredients with ice and strain into a cocktail glass.

Canadian Cherry

1½ fl. oz. (45 ml) Canadian whisky   ½ fl. oz. (15 ml) cherry brandy
½ tsp fresh lemon juice   ½ tsp fresh orange juice

Shake ingredients with ice. Strain into an ice-filled rocks glass.

2nd

Pineapple Batida

2 fl. oz. (60 ml) cachaça   3 tbsp pineapple chunks
2 fl. oz. (60 ml) coconut milk   2 tsp honey
1 cup ice

Blend all the ingredients with the ice and pour into a highball glass.

3rd

Piccadilly

1½ fl. oz. (45 ml) gin   ¾ fl. oz. (22 ml) dry vermouth
Dash grenadine   Dash pastis

Mix ingredients with ice and strain into a cocktail glass.

4th **Independence Day** (USA)

American Beauty

¾ fl. oz. (22 ml) brandy   ¾ fl. oz. (22 ml) orange juice
½ fl. oz. (15 ml) dry vermouth   ¼ tsp white crème de menthe
¼ tsp grenadine   ½ fl. oz. (15 ml) port

Shake all the ingredients, except the port, with ice and strain into a cocktail glass. Float the port over the drink.

American Glory

2 fl. oz. (60 ml) orange juice   ¾ fl. oz. (22 ml) grenadine
1 tsp lemon juice   Champagne

Add the ingredients to a champagne flute over ice. Top up with chilled champagne.

Lemon Cola Float (non-alcoholic)

2 scoops lemon sorbet   Cola

Add sorbet to a highball glass and top up with cola. Finish with a grating of lemon peel.

Canadian

Canadians and Scots spell their whisky without the 'e', unlike the Americans and Irish. Remember to use the appropriate country's whisky/whiskey for authentic cocktails.

5th ▶ Pimm's Royal

1½ fl. oz. (45 ml) Pimm's No 1
Champagne

Pour Pimm's into a small champagne flute. Top up with
champagne, then stir gently before finishing with a slice
of strawberry.

6th Citrus Martini

1 fl. oz. (30 ml) vodka
1 fl. oz. (30 ml) orange liqueur
1 fl. oz. (30 ml) grapefruit juice

Shake ingredients with ice and strain into a cocktail glass. Finish
with a twist of orange.

7th Fresh Lime & Ginger Soda

(non-alcoholic)

Juice 2 limes
3 tsp sugar
Pinch of salt
1 tsp freshly grated ginger
Soda water

Muddle the lime juice, sugar, salt, and ginger, then strain into a
highball glass over ice. Top up with soda water.

8th Classic Raki

1½ fl. oz. (45 ml) raki   Still mineral water

Pour raki over ice in a lowball glass and top up with mineral
water to taste.

9th Newton's Apple

1½ fl. oz. (45 ml) calvados
¾ fl. oz. (22 ml) triple sec
2 dashes Angostura bitters

Mix ingredients with ice and strain into a cocktail glass.

10th Derby

2 fl. oz. (60 ml) gin   1 tsp peach bitters

Mix ingredients with ice and strain into a cocktail glass. Finish
off with a sprig of mint.

11th Lemon Meringue Pie

1½ fl. oz. (45 ml) white rum
1 fl. oz. (30 ml) lemon juice
2 scoops vanilla ice cream

Blend ingredients until smooth and serve in a cocktail glass.

Pimm's Royal

Pimm's has become the classic summer drink. This is a great cocktail for parties – the champagne can be substituted with sparkling wine.

12th Mango Lassi (non-alcoholic)

1 peeled and chopped mango
3 fl. oz. (90 ml) milk
2 fl. oz. (60 ml) yoghurt
1 tsp sugar

Blend ingredients until smooth. Serve in a highball glass over ice.

13th Star Cocktail

1½ fl. oz. (45 ml) apple brandy
¾ fl. oz. (22 ml) dry vermouth
Dash Angostura bitters

Mix ingredients together with ice and strain into a cocktail glass.

14th Bastille Day

▶ Kir

2 tsp crème de cassis
Chilled dry white wine to fill

Add ingredients to a wine glass. Stir.

French Rose

1 fl. oz. (30 ml) gin
½ fl. oz. (15 ml) cherry brandy
½ fl. oz. (15 ml) cherry liqueur

Shake ingredients with crushed ice. Strain into a cocktail glass.

15th Panama

1½ fl. oz. (45 ml) Jamaican rum   ½ fl. oz. (15 ml) crème de cacao
½ fl. oz. (15 ml) cream

Shake ingredients well with ice and strain into a cocktail glass.

16th Fuzzy Navel

1½ fl. oz. (45 ml) peach schnapps
½ fl. oz. (15 ml) vodka
Orange juice to fill

Pour ingredients over ice in a highball glass and stir. Garnish
with a single slice of orange.

17th Zanzibar

1 fl. oz. (30 ml) gin
1 fl. oz. (30 ml) dry vermouth
¾ fl. oz. (22 ml) lemon juice
1 tsp sugar syrup

Shake ingredients with ice and strain into a cocktail glass. Serve
with a twist of lemon.

Kir

Crème de cassis is a blackcurrant liqueur and is a must for the classic Kir or the sparkling Kir Royale.

18th Coffee Freeze (non-alcoholic)

1 scoop vanilla ice cream   Cold coffee to fill

Mix ice cream and coffee in a rocks glass, then garnish with a
pinch of cinnamon.

19th Devil's Punchbowl

1½ fl. oz. (45 ml) vodka
½ fl. oz. (15 ml) crème de cassis
½ fl. oz. (15 ml) lime juice
Ginger ale

Pour ingredients over ice in a highball glass. Top up with ginger
ale. Finish with a wedge of lime.

20th Tequila Sunrise

1½ fl. oz. (45 ml) tequila
¾ fl. oz. (22 ml) grenadine
3 fl. oz. (90 ml) orange juice

Mix orange and tequila with ice in a highball glass. Float the
grenadine on top. Finish with a slice of orange on the rim of
the glass.

21st Old Pal

¾ fl. oz. (22 ml) bourbon   ¾ fl. oz. (22 ml) Campari
¾ fl. oz. (22 ml) dry vermouth

Stir ingredients with ice and strain into a cocktail glass.

22nd Xanthia

¾ fl. oz. (22 ml) gin
¾ fl. oz. (22 ml) Yellow Chartreuse
¾ fl. oz. (22 ml) cherry brandy

Mix ingredients with ice and strain into a cocktail glass.

23rd ▶ Banana Colada

1 fl. oz. (30 ml) dark rum
1 fl. oz. (30 ml) light rum
1 banana
1 fl. oz. (30 ml) coconut cream
4 fl. oz. (120 ml) pineapple juice

Mix in a blender until smooth. Pour into a highball glass over ice.

24th Kir Raspberry

1 fl. oz. (30 ml) Chambord
Champagne

Add Chambord to a champagne flute and then top up with
chilled champagne.

Banana Colada

This is one great way to ensure you eat your fruit. You can omit the rum for a Virgin Banana Colada.

25th Rum Bay Breeze

1½ fl. oz. (45 ml) white rum   2 fl. oz. (60 ml) pineapple juice
2 fl. oz. (60 ml) cranberry juice

Pour ingredients over ice in a highball glass. Stir. Finish with a
cube of pineapple and a cherry on a cocktail stick.

26th White Lady

¾ fl. oz. (22 ml) Cointreau
¾ fl. oz. (22 ml) gin
¾ fl. oz. (22 ml) fresh lemon juice
Dash sugar syrup
Dash egg white

Shake ingredients with ice and strain into a cocktail glass.

27th Campari Cocktail

1 fl. oz. (30 ml) Campari   ¾ fl. oz. (22 ml) vodka
Dash Angostura bitters

Shake ingredients with ice and strain into a cocktail glass.
Garnish with a twist of lemon.

28th ▶ Mexican Grasshopper

1 fl. oz. (30 ml) white crème de menthe
1 fl. oz. (30 ml) Kahlua
1 fl. oz. (30 ml) cream

Mix ingredients with ice and strain into a cocktail glass.

29th Bronx

1½ fl. oz. (45 ml) gin
½ fl. oz. (15 ml) sweet vermouth
½ fl. oz. (15 ml) dry vermouth
2 fl. oz. (60 ml) orange juice
Dash Angostura bitters

Combine ingredients in a shaker with ice. Strain into a cocktail
glass. Finish with a slice of orange.

30th Vermouth Cocktail

1¼ fl. oz. (37 ml) dry vermouth
1¼ fl. oz. (37 ml) sweet vermouth
Dash orange bitters

Shake ingredients with ice and strain into a cocktail glass.

31st Brandy Puff

1½ fl. oz. (45 ml) brandy   2 fl. oz. (60 ml) milk
Soda

Shake the brandy and milk with ice. Strain over ice in a rocks
glass. Top up with soda.

Mexican Grasshopper

Kahlua is a Mexican coffee liqueur and is a very versatile ingredient that can be used in cocktails such as the White Russian and Black Russian.

1st Valencia

1/2 fl. oz. (15 ml) apricot brandy   1 fl. oz. (30 ml) orange juice
Sparkling wine

Shake ingredients with ice and strain into a champagne flute. Top up with sparkling wine. Finish with a maraschino cherry.

2nd Margarita

1 1/2 fl. oz. (45 ml) tequila
1/2 fl. oz. (15 ml) triple sec
1 fl. oz. (30 ml) lime juice

Shake with ice and strain into a salt-rimmed margarita glass.

3rd Blue Lagoon

2 1/2 fl. oz. (15 ml) vodka   1/2 fl. oz. (15 ml) blue curaçao
Lemonade to fill

Mix ingredients with ice in a highball glass, then finish with a slice of lime.

4th ▶ New Orleans Fizz

1 1/2 fl. oz. (45 ml) gin   1/2 fl. oz. (15 ml) lime juice
1/2 fl. oz. (15 ml) lemon juice   1/2 fl. oz. (15 ml) sugar
1/4 fl. oz. (7 ml) cream   1 egg white
3 dashes orange flower water

Shake ingredients with ice. Strain into a highball glass over ice.

5th Lemon Kentucky

1 1/2 fl. oz. (45 ml) bourbon   Bitter lemon to top up

Pour ingredients over ice cubes in a highball glass and then top up with bitter lemon.

6th Irish Martini

1 1/2 fl. oz. (45 ml) Irish whiskey   1/2 fl. oz. (15 ml) dry vermouth
1/2 fl. oz. (15 ml) sweet vermouth

Mix ingredients with ice and strain into a cocktail glass. Finish off with a twist of lemon.

7th Batida De Coco

2 fl. oz. (60 ml) cachaça
3 fl. oz. (90 ml) coconut milk
2 tsp sugar
2 fl. oz. (60 ml) sweetened condensed milk

Blend ingredients with ice and strain into a cocktail glass.

Your Own Special Occasions and Cocktail Ratings

New Orleans Fizz

This cocktail, also known as the Ramos Gin Fizz, was invented in New Orleans in the late 1800s. The orange flower water is a must.

8th **Prince of Wales**

1/2 fl. oz. (15 ml) brandy
1/2 fl. oz. (15 ml) Madeira
1/4 fl. oz. (7 ml) orange curaçao
Dash Angostura bitters
Champagne

Shake the brandy, Madeira, orange curaçao, and Angostura bitters
with ice. Strain into a cocktail glass. Top up with champagne.

9th **Screwdriver**

1 1/2 fl. oz. (45 ml) vodka
Fresh orange juice to fill

Pour into an ice-filled highball glass. Stir.

10th **Naked Lady**

1 fl. oz. (30 ml) rum
1/2 fl. oz. (15 ml) sweet vermouth
1/2 fl. oz. (15 ml) apricot brandy
Dash lemon juice
Dash grenadine

Shake ingredients with ice and strain into a cocktail glass.

11th **Claret Lemonade**

2 fl. oz. (60 ml) claret
Juice of a lemon
2 tsp sugar
Sparkling water

Pour ingredients into a highball glass over ice. Stir. Top up with
sparkling water.

12th ▶ **Death In The Afternoon**

1 fl. oz. (30 ml) Pernod   Chilled champagne
Pour Pernod into a champagne flute and top up with champagne.

13th **Canadian Summer**

1 fl. oz. (30 ml) Canadian whisky
3/4 fl. oz. (22 ml) green crème de menthe
Soda water

Stir the ingredients in a rocks glass with ice. Top up with
soda water.

14th **Queen Elizabeth**

1 1/2 fl. oz. (45 ml) gin
1/2 fl. oz. (15 ml) dry vermouth
1/2 fl. oz. (15 ml) Benedictine

Stir ingredients with ice and strain into a cocktail glass.

Death In The Afternoon

It's a sinister name for such a fine drink. Pernod is an anise-flavored drink, and became a successor to absinthe when it was outlawed.

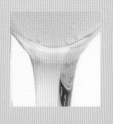

15th   Limoncello Martini

1½ fl. oz. (45 ml) vodka
½ fl. oz. (15 ml) limoncello
Dash Angostura bitters

Shake ingredients with ice and strain into a cocktail glass. Serve
with a twist of lemon.

16th   Kir Royale

2 tsp crème de cassis
Champagne to fill

Pour ingredients into a champagne flute and stir gently.

17th   The Big Apple

1½ fl. oz. (45 ml) calvados
¾ fl. oz. (22 ml) sweet red vermouth
2 fl. oz. (60 ml) apple juice
Soda water

Mix ingredients with ice and strain into an ice-filled highball
glass. Top up with soda water.

18th   Bitter Pill

1½ fl. oz. (45 ml) gin
¼ fl. oz. (7 ml) grenadine
Bitter lemon to fill

Mix ingredients with ice in a highball glass.

19th ▶ Foxtrot

1½ fl. oz. (45 ml) light rum
½ fl. oz. (15 ml) orange curaçao
¾ fl. oz. (22 ml) lemon juice

Shake all ingredients together with ice and then strain into a
cocktail glass.

20th   Chocolate Orange

1½ fl. oz. (45 ml) orange liqueur
2 scoops chocolate ice cream
Lemonade to fill

Add ingredients to a highball glass. Finish with a slice of orange.

21st   Berry Margarita

1½ fl. oz. (45 ml) tequila
½ fl. oz. (15 ml) crème de mure
½ fl. oz. (15 ml) fresh lemon juice

Shake ingredients with ice, then strain into a salt-rimmed
margarita glass.

Foxtrot

Curaçao is made from the peel of bitter oranges and can be colored orange, blue, green, or left clear.

22nd Cosmopolitan

1¼ fl. oz. (37 ml) vodka
¼ fl. oz. (7 ml) fresh lime juice
¼ fl. oz. (7 ml) triple sec
¼ fl. oz. (7 ml) cranberry juice

Shake ingredients with ice and strain into a cocktail glass. Finish
with a wedge of lime served on the rim of the glass.

23rd Tequila Sour

1½ fl. oz. (45 ml) tequila
2 fl. oz. (60 ml) lemon juice
1 tsp sugar

Shake ingredients with crushed ice and strain into a sours glass.

24th Astoria

1½ fl. oz. (45 ml) gin
¾ fl. oz. (22 ml) dry vermouth
Dash orange bitters

Mix with ice and strain into a cocktail glass. Finish with an olive.

25th Honeybee

1½ fl. oz. (45 ml) light rum
2 tsp fresh lemon juice
2 tsp honey

Shake ingredients with ice and strain into a cocktail glass.

26th Lemon Refresher

1 fl. oz. (30 ml) limoncello
Prosecco

Pour chilled limoncello into a champagne flute, then top up with
chilled prosecco.

27th Barbary Coast

1 fl. oz. (30 ml) Scotch
½ fl. oz. (15 ml) gin
½ fl. oz. (15 ml) light crème de cacao
½ fl. oz. (15 ml) cream

Shake ingredients with ice and strain into a cocktail glass.

28th ▶ Stinger

1½ fl. oz. (45 ml) brandy
¾ fl. oz. (22 ml) white crème de menthe

Shake ingredients with ice and strain into a cocktail glass.

Stinger

An unusual cocktail that combines minty liqueur with brandy. You may wish to adjust the amount of liqueur to your own taste.

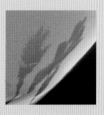

Holiday Specials

Damn The Weather

1 fl. oz. (30 ml) gin
$^1/_2$ fl. oz. (15 ml) sweet vermouth
$^1/_2$ fl. oz. (15 ml) orange juice
Dash triple sec

Shake ingredients with ice and strain into a cocktail glass.

Summer Holiday

1 fl. oz. (30 ml) brandy
Dash Angostura bitters

1 fl. oz. (30 ml) pineapple juice
Lemonade

Stir the brandy, pineapple juice and bitters with ice in a highball
glass. Top up with lemonade. Finish with a skewer of pineapple.

Sunshine

1$^1/_2$ fl. oz. (45 ml) gin
$^1/_2$ fl. oz. (15 ml) sweet vermouth
Dash aromatic bitters

Shake ingredients with ice and strain into a cocktail glass. Finish
with a twist of orange.

Bank Holiday Breeze

1 fl. oz. (30 ml) light rum
$^1/_2$ fl. oz. (15 ml) triple sec
1 fl. oz. (30 ml) cranberry juice
Soda water

Stir ingredients with ice in a highball glass. Top up with soda.

29th Sea Fizz

1$^1/_2$ fl. oz. (45 ml) absinthe
1 tsp sugar
Soda water

Juice of $^1/_2$ a lemon
1 egg white

Shake with ice and strain into a highball glass. Top up with soda.

30th ▶ Kamikaze

1$^1/_2$ fl. oz. (45 ml) vodka
1 fl. oz. (30 ml) Cointreau
1 fl. oz. (30 ml) lemon juice

Mix ingredients in a shaker with ice. Strain into a cocktail glass.

31st Madeira Flip

1$^1/_2$ fl. oz. (45 ml) Madeira
1 egg

2 tsp sugar syrup

Shake ingredients with ice. Strain into an ice-filled rocks glass.

Kamikaze

This is a more sophisticated version of the Kamikaze shot drink. You can also serve it on the rocks (pour the drink over ice in a rocks glass).

SEPTEMBER

First Monday Of September, Labor Day, USA

▶ American Grog

1½ fl. oz. (45 ml) bourbon   ½ fl. oz. (15 ml) lemon juice
1 tsp sugar   Hot water to fill

Add ingredients to a heatproof glass and stir.

Stars & Stripes

1 fl. oz. (30 ml) grenadine   1 fl. oz. (30 ml) maraschino liqueur
1 fl. oz. (30 ml) blue curaçao

Layer ingredients carefully in a pousse-café glass.

Boston Sidecar

¾ fl. oz (22 ml) light rum   ¾ fl. oz (22 ml) brandy
¾ fl. oz (22 ml) triple sec   ¾ fl. oz (22 ml) lime juice

Shake ingredients with ice and strain into a cocktail glass.

Chicago

¾ fl. oz (22 ml) brandy   Dash triple sec
Dash Angostura bitters   Champagne

Shake brandy, triple sec, and Angostura bitters with ice. Strain into a cocktail glass and top up with champagne.

California Lemonade

2 fl. oz. (60 ml) bourbon   1 fl. oz. (30 ml) lemon juice
1 tsp sugar   Soda water

Shake the bourbon, sugar, and lemon with ice. Strain into an ice-filled highball glass and top up with soda water.

1st Hollywood Martini

1½ fl. oz. (45 ml) gin   ½ fl. oz. (15 ml) Goldwasser
½ fl. oz. (15 ml) dry vermouth

Combine ingredients in a cocktail shaker with ice. Strain into a cocktail glass. Decorate with an olive.

2nd Vanilla Chiller

2 fl. oz. (60 ml) vodka   2 scoops vanilla ice cream
Lemonade to fill

Add ice cream to a highball glass. Add the vodka and lemonade. Decorate with a slice of lemon.

American Grog

Grog was originally made with rum and hot water, but this version uses bourbon for an all-American twist.

3rd   Brandy Zoom

1¹/₂ fl. oz. (45 ml) brandy
³/₄ fl. oz. (22 ml) cream
¹/₂ fl. oz. (15 ml) honey

Shake ingredients with ice and strain into a cocktail glass.

4th   French 75

1 fl. oz. (30 ml) gin   ¹/₂ fl. oz. (15 ml) lemon juice
1 tsp sugar   Champagne

Pour gin, lemon and sugar into a champagne flute. Stir. Add ice.
Top up with champagne.

5th   ▶ Old Nick

1¹/₂ fl. oz. (45 ml) Canadian whisky
¹/₂ fl. oz. (15 ml) Drambuie
¹/₂ fl. oz. (15 ml) orange juice
¹/₂ fl. oz. (15 ml) lemon juice
3 dashes orange bitters

Shake ingredients with ice, then strain into a rocks glass filled up
with ice.

6th   Apricot Lady

1 fl. oz. (30 ml) white rum   1 fl. oz. (30 ml) apricot brandy
¹/₂ fl. oz. (15 ml) orange liqueur   ¹/₂ fl. oz. (15 ml) lemon juice
1 egg white

Shake ingredients with ice. Strain into an ice-filled rocks glass.

7th   Sangrita

Serves 4

12 fl. oz. (360 ml) tomato juice   8 fl. oz. (240 ml) orange juice
2 tbsp lime juice   Tabasco sauce to taste
1 tbsp finely minced onion
1¹/₂ fl. oz. (45 ml) tequila in a shot glass per person

Blend ingredients until smooth. Strain into ice-filled rocks
glasses. Drink, alternating with sips of tequila.

8th   Lime Mimosa

¹/₂ fl. oz. (15 ml) simple syrup   Juice 1 lime
Champagne

Pour the lime juice and syrup into a champagne flute. Top up with
chilled champagne.

9th   Greyhound

2 fl. oz. (60 ml) vodka
4 fl. oz. (120 ml) grapefruit juice

Pour ingredients into a highball glass with ice and stir well.

Old Nick

Drambuie is a Scotch-based liqueur flavored with
heather, honey, and herbs. Bonnie Prince Charlie is said
to have given the recipe to the MacKinnon family in 1745.

10th Orange Lemonade (non-alcoholic)

2 fl. oz. (60 ml) orange juice
³/₄ fl. oz. (22 ml) lemon juice
³/₄ fl. oz. (22 ml) sugar syrup
Soda water

Mix with ice in a large rocks glass. Top up with soda water.

11th Spritzer

4 fl. oz. (120 ml) white wine   Soda water

Pour the wine into an ice-filled highball glass and top up with
soda water. Finish with a wheel of lemon.

12th ▶ Long Island Iced Tea

¹/₂ fl. oz. (15 ml) vodka   ¹/₂ fl. oz. (15 ml) gin
¹/₂ fl. oz. (15 ml) white rum   ¹/₂ fl. oz. (15 ml) tequila
¹/₂ tsp lemon juice   ¹/₂ tsp sugar
Cola

Mix ingredients with ice in a highball glass. Top up with cola.

13th Strawberry Fizz

1 fl. oz. (30 ml) gin   1 fl. oz. (30 ml) strawberry liqueur
1 tsp sugar syrup   Soda water

Combine ingredients in a highball glass with ice. Top up with soda
and finish with a strawberry slice and a sprig of mint.

14th B-52

³/₄ fl. oz. (22 ml) Kahlua
³/₄ fl. oz. (22 ml) Baileys Irish Cream
³/₄ fl. oz. (22 ml) Grand Marnier

In a shot glass or pousse-café glass, carefully layer ingredients
by pouring each one over the back of a spoon; this will help
prevent the layers from mixing. Start with Kahlua, then Irish
Cream, and finish with Grand Marnier.

15th Hazelnut Martini

1¹/₂ fl. oz. (45 ml) vodka
¹/₂ fl. oz. (15 ml) Frangelico

Shake ingredients with ice. Strain into a cocktail glass.

16th Southern Peach

1 fl. oz. (30 ml) Southern Comfort
1 fl. oz. (30 ml) bourbon
¹/₄ fl. oz. (7 ml) peach brandy
Soda

Pour ingredients into an ice-filled rocks glass. Top up with soda.

Long Island Iced Tea

There's no tea – just a lot of booze. The Long Island Iced Tea has become an all-time favorite throughout the world.

17th Dutch Martini

1¹/₂ fl. oz. (45 ml) genever
¹/₂ fl. oz. (15 ml) dry vermouth

Shake ingredients with ice and strain into a cocktail glass. Finish
with a twist of orange.

18th Horse's Neck

2 fl. oz. (60 ml) brandy
Ginger ale to fill

Place a spiral of lemon in a highball glass, securing one end to
the rim of the glass. Pour in the brandy. Add ice and the ginger
ale to taste.

19th Dark & Stormy

2 fl. oz. (60 ml) rum   3 fl. oz. (90 ml) ginger beer

Pour ingredients into an ice-filled highball glass. Finish with a
wedge of lime.

20th Carol Channing

1 tsp raspberry liqueur
1 tsp raspberry eau de vie
Dash sugar syrup
Champagne

Shake ingredients with ice. Strain into a champagne flute. Top up
with champagne.

21st Grenadine Cooler (non-alcoholic)

1 fl. oz. (30 ml) non-alcoholic grenadine
Ginger ale to top up

Add ingredients to a rocks glass filled with ice. Finish with an
orange slice and a cherry.

22nd Old Cuban

1 fl. oz. (30 ml) white rum
³/₄ fl. oz. (22 ml) fresh lime juice
1 fl. oz. (30 ml) simple syrup
2 dashes Angostura bitters
6 mint leaves
Champagne

Muddle lime juice, syrup, and mint. Shake with the rum, bitters,
and ice. Strain into a cocktail glass and top up with champagne.

23rd ▶ Royal

1¹/₂ fl. oz. (45 ml) gin   ¹/₂ tsp sugar
Juice ¹/₂ lime   1 egg yolk

Shake ingredients with ice and strain into a cocktail glass.

Royal

Recipes with egg need to be shaken slightly longer
than other cocktails to blend all the ingredients
together properly.

24th **Rum Warmer**

1¼ fl. oz. (7 ml) dark rum   Hot tea to fill

Pour ingredients into a heatproof glass. Finish with a layer of whipped cream.

25th ▶ **Cinnamon Apple**

1 fl. oz. (30 ml) cinnamon schnapps
Hot cider to fill

Pour ingredients into a heatproof glass. Finish with a cinnamon stick as a stirrer.

26th **Autumn Virgin** (non-alcoholic)

3 fl. oz. (90 ml) apple juice   1 tsp sugar syrup
Soda water to fill

Run a lime wedge around the edge of a highball glass and dip the glass into a saucer of brown sugar. Add the juice and sugar. Stir. Add soda and ice.

27th **Danish Martini**

1½ fl. oz. (45 ml) aquavit
½ fl. oz. (15 ml) dry vermouth

Shake ingredients with ice and strain into a cocktail glass. Garnish with an olive.

28th **Mae West**

1½ fl. oz. (45 ml) brandy   1 egg yolk
1 tsp sugar

Shake ingredients with ice and strain into a cocktail glass, then top up with a sprinkling of cayenne pepper.

29th **Genoa Cocktail**

¾ fl. oz. (22 ml) gin
¾ fl. oz. (22 ml) grappa
2 tsp sambuca
2 tsp dry vermouth

Mix ingredients with ice. Strain into a cocktail glass.

30th **Caesar**

1 fl. oz. (30 ml) vodka
4 fl. oz. (120 ml) Clamato juice
Salt and pepper
Dash Worcestershire sauce
Dash Tabasco sauce

Run a lime around the rim of a highball glass and dip it in to a saucer of celery salt. Shake ingredients with ice. Strain into the highball glass filled with ice.

Cinnamon Apple

An unusual take on the classic mix of cinnamon and apple. Cinnamon schnapps and cider make a great combination for autumn.

OCTOBER

1st — Apple Tart

1½ fl. oz. (45 ml) calvados
½ fl. oz. (15 ml) sweet red vermouth
Dash Angostura bitters
Tonic water to fill

Mix ingredients with ice in a highball glass. Perch a slice of lemon on the rim.

2nd — Sloe Gin Cocktail

2 fl. oz. (60 ml) sloe gin
¼ tsp dry vermouth
Dash orange bitters

Shake ingredients with ice and strain into a cocktail glass.

3rd — Peach Fizz (non-alcoholic)

1 peach puréed
Dash non-alcoholic grenadine
2 tsp sugar syrup
Soda water

Add the peach purée and syrup to a highball glass. Stir. Top up with soda and ice. Finish with a couple of raspberries.

4th — Drambuie & Soda

2 fl. oz. (60 ml) Drambuie
Soda

Pour Drambuie into an ice-filled rocks glass. Top up with soda. Finish with a twist of lime.

5th — Sweet Maria

1 fl. oz. (30 ml) vodka
1 tbsp cream
½ fl. oz. (15 ml) amaretto

Shake ingredients with ice and strain into a cocktail glass.

6th — Gin & Sin

1½ fl. oz. (45 ml) gin
¾ fl. oz. (22 ml) orange juice
¾ fl. oz. (22 ml) lemon juice
½ tsp grenadine

Shake ingredients with ice and strain into a cocktail glass.

7th — Highland Sling

2 fl. oz. (60 ml) Scotch whisky
1 tsp sugar
1 fl. oz. (30 ml) lemon juice
2 tsp water

Shake ingredients with ice and strain into a rocks glass over ice.

Your Own Special Occasions and Cocktail Ratings

Highland Sling

The Scotch whisky combined with tart lemon and sugar
makes a great cocktail in this version of a sling.

8th ▶ Deauville

$1/2$ fl. oz. (15 ml) calvados
$1/2$ fl. oz. (15 ml) brandy
$1/2$ fl. oz. (15 ml) triple sec
Juice of $1/4$ lemon

Shake ingredients with ice and strain into a cocktail glass.

9th Iced Coffee

$1^1/2$ fl. oz. (45 ml) Kahlua
Cold coffee to fill

Mix ingredients over ice in a highball glass.

10th Dry Rob Roy

$1^1/2$ fl. oz. (45 ml) whiskey
$1/4$ fl. oz. (7 ml) dry vermouth
Dash Angostura bitters

Stir ingredients with ice and strain into a cocktail glass. Finish
with a twist of lemon.

11th Amber

1 fl. oz. (30 ml) light rum
$3/4$ fl. oz. (22 ml) sweet red vermouth
1 tsp lemon juice
Dash orange bitters

Shake ingredients with ice and strain into a cocktail glass.

12th Gin Swizzle

$1^1/2$ fl. oz. (45 ml) gin
2 fl. oz. (60 ml) lime juice
2 fl. oz. (60 ml) soda water
1 tsp sugar

Stir ingredients in a highball glass over ice. Finish with a
lime wheel.

13th Rosemary Martini

$1^1/2$ fl. oz. (45 ml) vodka
$1/2$ fl. oz. (15 ml) dry vermouth
1 sprig rosemary

Stir ingredients with ice and strain into a cocktail glass. Finish
with the rosemary.

14th Ferrari on the Rocks

1 fl. oz. (30 ml) dry vermouth
$1/2$ fl. oz. (15 ml) amaretto
Dash Angostura bitters

Shake ingredients with ice. Strain into an ice-filled rocks glass.

Deauville

Calvados is a much-respected apple brandy made in France. Buy for the cocktail cabinet and also enjoy on its own as a digestif.

15th Abbey Cocktail

1¹/₂ fl. oz. (45 ml) gin   Dash orange bitters
1 fl. oz. (30 ml) orange juice

Shake ingredients with ice and strain into a cocktail glass.

16th Rum Comfort

³/₄ fl. oz. (22 ml) light rum   ³/₄ fl. oz. (22 ml) Southern Comfort
2 fl. oz. (60 ml) orange juice   1¹/₂ fl. oz. (45 ml) pineapple juice
2 tsp lemon juice

Shake ingredients with ice and strain into a highball glass over
crushed ice. Finish with a slice of orange.

17th Flirtini

2 pieces fresh pineapple   ¹/₂ fl. oz. (15 ml) vodka
¹/₂ fl. oz. (15 ml) orange liqueur   1 fl. oz. (30 ml) pineapple juice
Champagne

Muddle pineapple and orange liqueur in a mixing glass. Add
vodka and pineapple juice. Stir. Strain into a cocktail glass and
top up with champagne.

18th Aberdeen Angus

1¹/₂ fl. oz. (45 ml) Scotch whisky   1 fl. oz. (30 ml) Drambuie
1 tbsp lime juice   1 tbsp honey

In a heatproof glass or mug, stir Scotch whisky and honey with a
little hot water until smooth. Add the lime juice. Warm the
Drambuie in a ladle and ignite, then pour it over the drink. Add
hot water to taste and stir before serving.

19th ▶ Sherry Refresher

3 fl. oz. (90 ml) sherry   2 fl. oz. (60 ml) soda water
1 tsp sugar syrup   1 tsp orange juice

Add ingredients to an ice-filled wine glass. Stir. Finish with a twist
of lemon.

20th Unfuzzy Navel (non-alcoholic)

6 fl. oz. (180 ml) orange juice   2 fl. oz. (60 ml) peach nectar

Pour ingredients over ice in a highball glass and stir.

21st Brandy Crusta

1¹/₂ fl. oz. (45 ml) brandy
¹/₂ fl. oz. (15 ml) orange curaçao
¹/₄ fl. oz. (7 ml) maraschino liqueur
¹/₄ fl. oz. (7 ml) fresh lemon juice
Dash aromatic bitters

Line a sugar-rimmed cocktail glass with a spiral of lemon peel.
Stir ingredients with ice and strain into the glass.

Sherry Refresher

Sherry mixed with soda water makes for a light cocktail, particularly suitable as a pre-lunch drink.

22nd Mojito

2 fl. oz. (60 ml) light rum
8 mint leaves
Soda

4 sugar cubes
4 wedges of lime

Muddle the mint, sugar, and limes in a highball glass. Add the ice
and rum, then top up with soda. Finish with a mint sprig.

23rd Pear Fizz

1 fl. oz. (30 ml) eau de vie Poire Williams
Champagne

Add the Poire Williams to a champagne flute, then top up
with champagne.

24th Ginger Martini

1$\frac{1}{2}$ fl. oz. (45 ml) vodka
1in chunk of fresh ginger
1 tsp sugar
Juice $\frac{1}{4}$ lime

Run the ginger around the rim of a cocktail glass then add the
ginger to the shaker. Shake all the ingredients with ice and strain
into the glass. Finish with a twist of lime.

25th ▶ Brandy Eggnog

1 fl. oz. (30 ml) brandy
$\frac{1}{2}$ fl. oz. (15 ml) sugar syrup

1$\frac{1}{4}$ fl. oz. (7 ml) milk
1 egg yolk

Shake ingredients thoroughly with ice and then strain into an
old-fashioned glass to drink.

26th Highland Cooler

2 fl. oz. (60 ml) Scotch whisky
$\frac{1}{2}$ tsp sugar
Soda water to taste

In a highball glass, dissolve the sugar with a splash of water. Add
the Scotch whisky and ice, then top up with water.

27th Rose Cocktail

1 fl. oz. (30 ml) dry vermouth
$\frac{1}{4}$ fl. oz. (7 ml) grenadine

1 fl. oz. (30 ml) kirsch

Mix ingredients with ice and strain into a cocktail glass. Finish
with a cherry perched on the rim of the glass.

28th Union Jack

1$\frac{1}{2}$ fl. oz. (45 ml) sloe gin
1 tsp grenadine

$\frac{1}{2}$ fl. oz. (15 ml) gin

Mix ingredients together with ice and then strain into a
cocktail glass.

Brandy Eggnog

Eggnog is traditionally a holiday drink and people in countries around the world use it to toast each other's health.

29th Night Cap

2 fl. oz. (60 ml) light rum   1 tsp sugar
Warm milk to fill

Mix ingredients in a heatproof glass. Sprinkle nutmeg on top.

30th Hot Chocolate Almond

1 fl. oz. (30 ml) butterscotch schnapps
$^1/_2$ fl. oz. (15 ml) amaretto
Hot chocolate to fill

Pour ingredients into a heatproof glass and then serve with
whipped cream.

31st Halloween

Witch's Eyeballs

2 fl. oz. (60 ml) vodka   2 fl. oz. (60 ml) cranberry juice
Lemonade   2 peeled lychees

Shake the vodka and cranberry with ice and pour into a highball
glass. Add the peeled lychees to the drink. Top up with lemonade.

▶ Monster

2 fl. oz. (60 ml) green crème de menthe
$^1/_2$ fl. oz. (15 ml) tequila

Shake ingredients with ice and strain into a cocktail glass.

Black Cat

2 fl. oz. (60 ml) Kahlua
$^1/_2$ fl. oz. (15 ml) vodka
Cola to fill

Mix ingredients with ice in a highball glass. Finish with a stick of
licorice as a stirrer!

Corpse Reviver

1 fl. oz. (30 ml) brandy
1 fl. oz. (30 ml) sweet vermouth
1 fl. oz. (30 ml) calvados

Shake ingredients with ice and strain into a cocktail glass.

Nightmare

1 fl. oz. (30 ml) gin
$^1/_2$ fl. oz. (15 ml) Dubonnet
$^1/_2$ fl. oz. (15 ml) cherry brandy
$^1/_2$ fl. oz. (15 ml) orange juice

Shake ingredients with ice and strain into a cocktail glass.

Monster

A creepy green cocktail, ideal for a Hallowe'en party. Pop in some skewers of grape 'eyeballs' if you wish to add to the effect!

NOVEMBER

1st — All Saints' Day

▶ Saintly (non-alcoholic)

2 fl. oz. (60 ml) raspberry juice   2 fl. oz. (60 ml) orange juice
Soda water
Pour ingredients over ice in a highball glass, then top up with soda water.

2nd — All Souls' Day
(Day of the Dead)

Angel's Kiss

1½ fl. oz. (45 ml) crème de cacao   Lightly whipped cream
Pour the crème de cacao into a liqueur glass. Finish with the cream and a cherry.

3rd — Blue Cosmopolitan

1½ fl. oz. (45 ml) vodka   1 fl. oz. (30 ml) blue curaçao
1 fl. oz. (30 ml) grapefruit juice   1 fl. oz. (30 ml) lime juice
Shake ingredients with ice and strain into a cocktail glass.

4th — Coconut Shake

1½ fl. oz. (45 ml) coconut rum   3 fl. oz. (90 ml) pineapple juice
2 fl. oz. (60 ml) cream   1 scoop vanilla ice cream
Blend with ice until smooth. Pour into a highball glass.

5th — Bonfire Night (UK)

Guy Fawkes Flamer

1½ fl. oz. (45 ml) vodka   Splash of 151 proof rum
Pour the vodka into a shot glass. Add the rum, ignite, and blow out the flame before drinking!

Fireworks

1 fl. oz. (30 ml) tequila   1 fl. oz. (30 ml) Goldschlager
Pour chilled tequila into a shot glass, then add the Goldschlager.

Gunpowder

1 fl. oz. (30 ml) gin   Dash sugar syrup
Dash lemon juice   Beer
Stir gin, sugar, and lemon in a highball glass. Top up with beer.

Saintly

A refreshing non-alcoholic drink for the more saintly among us. You can top it up with lemonade for an even sweeter version.

6th ▶ Widow's Kiss

1 fl. oz. (30 ml) apple brandy
³/₄ fl. oz. (22 ml) Yellow Chartreuse
³/₄ fl. oz. (22 ml) Benedictine
Dash bitters
Shake ingredients with ice and strain into a cocktail glass.

7th The Aviation

1¹/₂ fl. oz. (45 ml) gin
1 fl. oz. (30 ml) lemon juice
1 fl. oz. (30 ml) maraschino liqueur
Shake ingredients with ice and strain into a cocktail glass.

8th Tropical Drambuie

1¹/₂ fl. oz. (45 ml) Drambuie
³/₄ fl. oz. (22 ml) light rum
2³/₄ fl. oz. (22 ml) passion-fruit juice

Mix Drambuie and rum with ice cubes in a highball glass. Top up
with passion-fruit juice and stir. Perch a slice of lemon on the rim
of the glass.

9th Tequini

1¹/₂ fl. oz. (45 ml) tequila
¹/₂ fl. oz. (15 ml) dry vermouth

Stir in a mixing glass with ice and strain into a cocktail glass.
Finish with a lemon twist.

10th Red Eye

¹/₂ glass of beer   1 fl. oz. (30 ml) vodka
1 fl. oz. (30 ml) tomato juice   1 egg

Pour the vodka into a beer glass with the beer and top up with
tomato juice. Crack in the egg but don't stir.

11th Mint Julep

1¹/₂ fl. oz. (45 ml) bourbon   4 mint sprigs
2 sugar cubes

Muddle the mint and sugar in a frosted julep cup or rocks glass.
Fill with crushed ice and pour the bourbon over the top.

12th The Pegu Club

1¹/₂ fl. oz. (45 ml) gin
³/₄ fl. oz. (22 ml) fresh lime juice
¹/₂ fl. oz (15 ml) Cointreau
Dash Angostura bitters
Dash orange bitters
Shake ingredients with ice and strain into a cocktail glass.

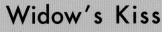

Widow's Kiss

Chartreuse is a plant-based liqueur made entirely from natural ingredients. Distilled only by the Chartreuse monks, its recipe is something of a secret.

13th Adios Amigos

1 fl. oz. (30 ml) light rum
1/2 fl. oz. (15 ml) dry vermouth
1/2 fl. oz. (15 ml) brandy
1/2 fl. oz. (15 ml) gin
3/4 fresh lime juice

Stir ingredients with ice and strain into a cocktail glass.

14th San Francisco

3/4 fl. oz. (22 ml) sloe gin
3/4 fl. oz. (22 ml) sweet vermouth
3/4 fl. oz. (22 ml) dry vermouth
Dash orange bitters
Dash Angostura bitters

Mix with ice, strain into a cocktail glass, and serve with a cherry.

15th Kentucky Mule

1 1/2 fl. oz. (45 ml) bourbon   3/4 fl. oz. (22 ml) Benedictine

Shake ingredients with ice and strain into a cocktail glass.

16th Rhythm & Blues

3/4 fl. oz. (22 ml) blue curaçao
3/4 fl. oz. (22 ml) coconut rum
3 tsp peach liqueur
3 tsp pineapple juice

Shake ingredients with ice. Strain into a highball glass over ice.

17th ▶ Alfonso

1 fl. oz. (30 ml) Dubonnet   1 sugar lump
Dash Angostura bitters   Champagne

Soak sugar lump in the Angostura bitters. Add ice to a
champagne flute, then add the Dubonnet. Top up with
champagne. Finish with a twist of lemon.

18th Emerson Martini

1 fl. oz. (30 ml) gin
3/4 fl. oz. (22 ml) sweet vermouth
1/2 fl. oz. (15 ml) maraschino liqueur
1/2 fl. oz. (15 ml) lemon juice

Shake ingredients with ice and strain into a cocktail glass.

19th Honeymoon

1 1/2 fl. oz. (45 ml) brandy   1 fl. oz. (30 ml) triple sec
1 tsp honey   1 tsp lemon

Shake all the ingredients with ice. Strain into a cocktail glass.
Finish with an orange slice on the rim of the glass.

Alfonso

Dubonnet, with its flavors of quinine and spices, makes an excellent apéritif.

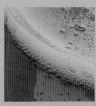

20th Frozen Margarita

1¹/₂ fl. oz. (45 ml) tequila
1 fl. oz. (30 ml) triple sec
1 fl. oz. (30 ml) lime juice

Run a lime along the rim of a margarita glass. Dip the rim in a
saucer of coarse sea salt. Put the ingredients in a blender with a
cup of crushed ice. Blend thoroughly.

21st Cherry Daiquiri

1 fl. oz. (30 ml) light rum
³/₄ fl. oz. (22 ml) cherry brandy
³/₄ fl. oz. (22 ml) lime juice
2 tsp kirsch

Mix ingredients with ice and strain into a cocktail glass.

22nd Vodka Martini

2 fl. oz. (60 ml) vodka
¹/₂ fl. oz. (15 ml) dry vermouth

Stir the ingredients with ice and strain into a cocktail glass.
Finish with an olive.

23rd Sir Knight Cocktail

1 fl. oz. (30 ml) cognac
¹/₂ fl. oz. (15 ml) Cointreau
¹/₄ fl. oz. (7 ml) Yellow Chartreuse
Dash Angostura bitters

Shake ingredients with crushed ice. Strain into a cocktail glass.

24th Pendennis

1¹/₂ fl. oz. (45 ml) gin
³/₄ fl. oz. (22 ml) apricot brandy
2 dashes Peychaud's bitters
1 fl. oz. (30 ml) fresh lime juice

Shake ingredients with ice and strain into a cocktail glass.

25th Red Wine Flip

3 fl. oz. (90 ml) red wine   1 egg yolk
2 tsp sugar

Shake ingredients with ice and strain into a flip glass.

26th ▶ Blood & Sand

³/₄ fl. oz. (22 ml) Scotch whisky
³/₄ fl. oz. (22 ml) red vermouth
¹/₄ fl. oz. (7 ml) cherry brandy
1¹/₂ fl. oz. (45 ml) orange juice

Shake ingredients with ice and strain into a cocktail glass.

Blood & Sand

This cocktail from the 1920s is believed to have been
named after the Rudolph Valentino movie.

27th Tulip

1 fl. oz. (30 ml) apricot brandy   1/2 fl. oz. (15 ml) apple brandy
1/2 fl. oz. (15 ml) sweet vermouth   1/2 fl. oz. (15 ml) lemon juice

Shake ingredients with ice and strain into a cocktail glass.

Thanksgiving (USA)
(The fourth Thursday of November)

▶ All American Fizz

1 fl. oz. (30 ml) gin   1/2 fl. oz. (15 ml) brandy
1 fl. oz. (30 ml) lemon juice   Dash grenadine
Soda water

Mix ingredients in an ice-filled highball glass. Top up with
soda water.

Liberty

1 fl. oz. (30 ml) dark rum   1 fl. oz. (30 ml) applejack
Dash sugar syrup

Shake ingredients with ice and strain into a cocktail glass.

Americana

1/4 fl. oz. (7 ml) whiskey   Dash aromatic bitters
1/2 tsp sugar   Champagne

Shake the whiskey, bitters, and sugar with ice. Strain into a
champagne glass and top up with champagne. Add a peach slice.

28th Yale Martini

1 1/2 fl. oz. (45 ml) gin   1/2 fl. oz. (15 ml) dry vermouth
Dash Angostura bitters   1 tsp blue curaçao

Mix ingredients with ice and strain into a cocktail glass.

29th Champagne Celebration

1/2 fl. oz. (15 ml) Cointreau   1/2 fl. oz. (15 ml) brandy
Champagne

Add the ingredients to a champagne flute. Top up with champagne.

30th St Andrew's Day

Scotch Cobbler

2 fl. oz. (60 ml) Scotch whisky
3 fl. oz. (90 ml) soda
1 tsp sugar

In an old-fashioned glass, dissolve the sugar in the soda. Add the
Scotch whisky over ice and stir.

All American Fizz

Some recipes call for club soda, others soda water.
They are the same thing, as is seltzer water and
carbonated water.

1st ▶ Mulled Wine

Serves 6
1 bottle red wine	2 cinnamon sticks
1/4 tsp nutmeg	1/4 tsp ginger
1/4 cup sugar	6 slices lemon
6 cloves, studded in an orange	

Heat ingredients in a saucepan. Strain into heatproof glasses.

Your Own Special Occasions and Cocktail Ratings

2nd Cherry Sling

2 fl. oz. (60 ml) cherry brandy   1 1/4 fl. oz. (7 ml) fresh lemon juice
1/2 tsp sugar

Shake ingredients with ice and strain into a rocks glass over ice.

3rd December Cranberry

1 1/2 fl. oz. (45 ml) vodka   1 fl. oz. (30 ml) cranberry liqueur
1 fl. oz. (30 ml) orange juice

Shake ingredients with ice and strain into a cocktail glass.

4th Vermouth Cassis

2 fl. oz. (60 ml) dry vermouth   1/2 fl. oz. (15 ml) crème de cassis
Soda

Pour over ice in a rocks glass. Finish with a twist of lemon.

5th Tea Punch

Serves 6
6 fl. oz. (180 ml) dark rum	1 bottle red wine
2 cups black tea	4 tsp sugar
6 lemon slices, each studded with a clove	

Heat all the ingredients gently in a saucepan, then ladle into heatproof glasses. Serve each with a lemon slice.

6th Gin Zoom

2 fl. oz. (60 ml) gin   1/4 fl. oz. (7 ml) cream
1 tsp honey

Dissolve the honey with a little hot water, then shake all the ingredients with ice. Strain into a rocks glass over ice.

7th Poinsettia

1/2 fl. oz. (15 ml) triple sec   2 fl. oz. (60 ml) cranberry juice
Champagne

Pour triple sec and cranberry juice into a champagne flute. Top up with champage.

Mulled Wine

There is no better drink for a cold December than mulled wine, and the spices fill the kitchen with a wonderful aroma.

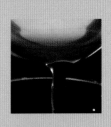

8th Desperate Housewife

1 fl. oz. (30 ml) gin
1 fl. oz. (30 ml) sherry
Soda water to fill

Pour ingredients over ice in a highball glass.

9th Italian Lemonade

1½ fl. oz. (45 ml) vodka
½ fl. oz. (15 ml) Campari
1 fl. oz. (30 ml) fresh lemon juice
1 tsp sugar
Soda water

Shake ingredients with ice and pour into a highball glass filled
with ice. Top up with soda water.

10th Pousse-Café

Maraschino liqueur   Orange curaçao
Green Chartreuse   Cognac

Layer ingredients equally into a pousse-café glass.

11th ▶ Cheat's Eggnog

1 fl. oz. (30 ml) bourbon
1 fl. oz. (30 ml) light rum
1 scoop vanilla ice cream

Stir ingredients together in a rocks glass until you have a
creamy consistency.

12th Hot Sangaree

2 fl. oz. (60 ml) brandy
1 tsp sugar dissolved in hot water
Hot water to fill

Add ingredients to a heatproof glass, then finish with a sprinkle of
nutmeg.

13th Japanese Slipper

1 fl. oz. (30 ml) melon liqueur
1 fl. oz. (30 ml) triple sec
1 fl. oz. (30 ml) lime juice
½ fl. oz. (15 ml) sugar syrup

Shake ingredients with ice and strain into a cocktail glass.

14th B&C

¾ fl. oz. (22 ml) Benedictine
¾ fl. oz. (22 ml) calvados

Pour Benedictine into a cocktail glass then add calvados.
Don't stir.

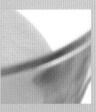

Cheat's Eggnog

This eggnog is ideal for those who won't want to eat raw eggs, and is so easy to make.

15th Glühwein

Serves 6

1 bottle red wine	6 fl. oz. (180 ml) brandy
2in slice fresh ginger	2 cinnamon sticks
4 tbsp sugar	1 orange, studded with six cloves

Gently heat all the ingredients, strain into heatproof glasses, and finish with orange slices.

16th Christmas Cheer (non-alcoholic)

Serves 6

2 cups apple juice	3 cups pineapple juice
2 cups cranberry juice	1 cinnamon stick
1/4 tsp nutmeg	Half a lemon

Gently heat ingredients in a saucepan. Strain into heatproof glasses and finish with a cinnamon stick as a stirrer.

17th Rum Cow

1½ fl. oz. (45 ml) dark rum	4 fl. oz. (120 ml) milk
2 drops vanilla essence	1 tsp sugar
Pinch nutmeg	

Shake ingredients with ice. Serve over ice in a highball glass.

18th Brandy Blazer

2 fl. oz. (60 ml) cognac   1 sugar cube

In a rocks glass, add the sugar and cognac and carefully ignite. Stir with a long-handled spoon until the flame is extinguished and finish with a twist of lemon.

19th John Collins

1½ fl. oz. (45 ml) bourbon	3/4 fl. oz. (22 ml) lemon juice
2 tsp sugar syrup	Soda water

Mix ingredients with ice in a Collins glass. Top up with soda. Finish with a cherry and orange slice.

20th La Habana

1 fl. oz. (30 ml) gin	1 fl. oz. (30 ml) apricot brandy
Juice ½ lime	

Shake ingredients with ice and strain into a cocktail glass over ice.

21st ▶ Snowball

1½ fl. oz. (45 ml) advocaat   ¼ fl. oz. (7 ml) fresh lemon juice
Lemonade

Pour the advocaat and lemon juice into an ice-filled highball glass. Top up with lemonade. Finish with a slice of lemon.

Snowball

It's a little old-fashioned, but the holiday season wouldn't be the same without a snowball made with advocaat.

22nd Almond Dream

1 fl. oz. (30 ml) coffee liqueur   1 fl. oz. (30 ml) amaretto
4 fl. oz. (120 ml) cream

Shake ingredients with ice and strain into a cocktail glass.

23rd Jack Frost

1½ fl. oz. (45 ml) gin
½ fl. oz. (15 ml) white crème de menthe
¼ fl. oz. (7 ml) cream

Shake ingredients with ice and strain into a cocktail glass.

24th Christmas Eve

Rum Eggnog

Serves 6
1½ fl. oz. (45 ml) dark rum   1 egg yolk
3 fl. oz. (90 ml) milk   1 fl. oz. (30 ml) cream

Shake ingredients with ice. Strain into an ice-filled highball glass.
Sprinkle with grated nutmeg.

25th Christmas Day

▶ Christmas Cracker

½ fl. oz. (15 ml) cherry brandy   Champagne

Add the ingredients to a champagne flute, top up with
champagne, then finish with a candied cherry.

Gold Champagne

1 tsp goldwasser
Champagne

Pour the gold-flecked goldwasser into a champagne flute and fill
with champagne.

Christmas Pudding

1 fl. oz. (30 ml) rum   1 fl. oz. (30 ml) Drambuie

Shake ingredients with ice and strain into a cocktail glass, then
finish with a couple of raisins.

26th Boxing Day

Buck's Fizz

Freshly squeezed orange juice   Champagne

Half-fill champagne flute with orange. Top up with champagne.

Christmas Cracker

Champagne is given a fruity twist with the addition of cherry brandy and a candied cherry.

27th Golden Cadillac

³/₄ fl. oz. (22 ml) white crème de cacao
³/₄ fl. oz. (22 ml) Galliano
³/₄ fl. oz. (22 ml) cream

Shake ingredients with ice and strain into a cocktail glass.

28th Hot White Wine Punch

Serves 6
6 fl. oz. (180 ml) brandy
1 bottle semi-dry white wine
Cinnamon stick
4 cloves

Heat the wine and spices gently in a saucepan. Strain into
heatproof glasses and pour over the brandy.

29th Irish Eyes

1 fl. oz. (30 ml) Irish whiskey   2 fl. oz. (60 ml) cream
¹/₂ fl. oz. (15 ml) green crème de menthe

Shake ingredients with ice and pour into an old-fashioned glass
over ice.

30th Ginger Snowball

2 fl. oz. (60 ml) advocaat
Ginger ale

Pour advocaat over ice in a rocks glass. Top up with ginger ale.

31st New Year's Eve

New Year Chill

1 fl. oz. (30 ml) vodka   1 fl. oz. (30 ml) amaretto
1 fl. oz. (30 ml) cream

Shake ingredients with ice and strain into a cocktail glass.

▶ Champagne Cocktail

1 sugar lump   Dash Angostura bitters
1 tsp brandy   Champagne

Douse sugar lump in Angostura bitters and add it with brandy to
a champagne flute. Top up with champagne.

Champanska

1 fl. oz. (30 ml) vodka
¹/₂ fl. oz. (15 ml) lime cordial
Champagne

Pour ingredients into a champagne flute. Stir gently. Finish with a
twist of lime.

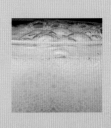

Champagne Cocktail

The champagne cocktail can be made with or without brandy – but as it's Christmas...

INDEX
BY DRINK TYPE

Brandy-based

Alexander	36
American Beauty	66
Apple Blossom	56
Apple Brandy Rickey	52
Apple Tart	96
Apple Turnover	44
Apricot Lady	88
B&B	54
B&C	118
B&P	22
Bentley	14
Between the Sheets	26
Big Apple, The	80
Boston Sidecar	86
Brandy Cassis	58
Brandy Cocktail	38
Brandy Crusta	100
Brandy Eggnog	102
Brandy Grog	10
Brandy Puff	74
Brandy Sling	34
Brandy Smash	16
Brandy Sour	18
Brandy Zoom	88
Calvados Sour	30
Celebration	50
Cherry Flip	42
Cherry Rum Fizz	8
Cherry Sling	116
Cognac & Mint Frappe	64
Corkscrew	14
Corpse Reviver	104
Country Gentleman	62
Deauville	98
French Connection	32
Honeymoon	110
Horse's Neck	92
Hot Sangaree	118
Lady Godiva	48
Mae West	94
Newton's Apple	68
Pick Me Up	40
Prince of Wales	78
Rolls Royce	60
Sidecar	20
Sir Knight Cocktail	112
Star Cocktail	70
Stinger	82
Summer Holiday	84
Tulip	114
Widow's Kiss	108
Xanthia	72

Tequila-based/ cachaça-based

Batida De Coco	76
Berry Margarita	80
Bloody Maria	54
Caipirinha	34
Depth Charge	48
El Diablo	30
Fireworks	106
Frozen Margarita	112
Long Island Iced Tea	90
Margarita	76

Mexican Colada	34
Pineapple Batida	66
Pineapple Margarita	44
Pomegranate Margarita	46
Sangrita	88
Tequila Screwdriver	24
Tequila Sour	82
Tequila Sunrise	72
Tequini	108

Whisky/Whiskey-based

Aberdeen Angus	100
American Grog	86
Balmoral	8
Barbary Coast	82
Blood & Sand	112
Bourbon Daisy	64
Brooklyn	20
California Lemonade	86
Canadian	66
Canadian Cherry	66
Canadian Summer	78
Cheat's Eggnog	118
Cola Float	32
Dry Rob Roy	98
Floater	62
Flying Scotsman	16
Frisco Sour	22
Godfather	28
Highland Cooler	102
Highland Sling	96
Irish Coffee	12
Irish Eyes	124
Irish Fix	30
Irish Martini	76
Irish Rose	30
John Collins	120
Kentucky Cocktail	38
Kentucky Mule	110
Lemon Kentucky	76
Manhattan	16
Mint Julep	108
Missouri Mule	52
Monte Carlo	26
New York	24
Old-Fashioned	14
Old Nick	88
Old Pal	72
Robbie Burns, The	14
St. Patrick's Day	30
Scotch Cobbler	114
South Coast	44
Southern Peach	90
Whiskey Collins	10
Whiskey Cooler	58
Whiskey Sangaree	60

Champagne-based/ wine-based

Alfonso	110
American Glory	66
Americana	114
Apple Turnover	44
Black Mountain Top	26
Black Pearl	8
Black Velvet	12

Blue Moon	28
Buck's Fizz	122
Campari Cocktail	74
Carol Channing	92
Champagne Celebration	114
Champagne Cocktail	124
Champagne Fizz	24
Champanska	124
Chicago	86
Christmas Cracker	122
Claret Lemonade	78
Death in the Afternoon	78
Flirtini	100
French 75	88
Glühwein	120
Gold Champagne	122
Hot White Wine Punch	124
Kir	70
Kir Raspberry	72
Kir Royale	80
Lemon Refresher	82
Lime Mimosa	88
Mimosa	34
Mulled Wine	116
Pear Champagne	38
Pear Fizz	102
Pick Me Up	40
Pimm's Royal	68
Poinsettia	116
Red Wine Cooler	28
Red Wine Flip	112
Sherry Refresher	100
Spritzer	90
Tinto de Verano	62
Trickster	36
Valencia	76
Valentine	20
White Lady	74
White Wine Cooler	52

Beer-based/cider-based

Black & Tan	60
Black Velvet	12
Cinnamon Apple	94
Depth Charge	48
Dog's Nose	44
Guinness Float	30
Hot Cider Cup	10
Red Eye	108

Non-alcoholic

Autumn Virgin	94
Christmas Cheer	120
Coffee Freeze	72
Detoxer	10
Fresh Lime & Ginger Soda	68
Grapefruit Refresher	36
Grenadine Cooler	92
Lemon Cola Float	66
Mango Lassi	70
Orange & Pineapple Flip	40
Orange Lemonade	90
Peach Fizz	96
Pomegranate Cooler	42
Prairie Oyster	44
Resolution	8

INDEX
ALPHABETICAL

Brandy Blazer	120	**D**			Godfather	28
Brandy Cassis	58	Daiquiri	24		Godmother	58
Brandy Cocktail	38	Damn the Weather	84		Gold Champagne	122
Brandy Crusta	100	Danish Martini	94		Golden Cadillac	124
Brandy Eggnog	102	Dark & Stormy	92		Grapefruit Refresher	36
Brandy Grog	10	Death in the Afternoon	78		Grasshopper	32
Brandy Puff	74	Deauville	98		Grenadine Cooler	92
Brandy Sling	34	December Cranberry	116		Greyhound	88
Brandy Smash	16	Depth Charge	48		Groundhog, The	18
Brandy Sour	18	Derby	68		Guinness Float	30
Brandy Zoom	88	Desperate Housewife	118		Gunpowder	106
Breakfast Martini	18	Detoxer	10		Guy Fawkes Flamer	106
Bronx	74	Devil's Punchbowl	72			
Brooklyn	20	Diplomat	60		**H**	
Buck's Fizz	122	Dirty Martini	48		Harvey Wallbanger	22
Bullshot	26	Dog's Nose	44		Havana Hot Chocolate	28
		Dragon, The	26		Hazelnut Martini	90
C		Drambuie & Soda	96		Hemingway Daiquiri	60
Caesar	94	Dry Martini	14		Highland Cooler	102
Caipirinha	34	Dry Rob Roy	98		Highland Sling	96
Caipirissima	38	Dutch Martini	92		Hollywood Martini	86
California Lemonade	86				Honeybee	82
Calvados Sour	30	**E**			Honeymoon	110
Campari & Soda	44	El Diablo	30		Horse's Neck	92
Campari Cocktail	74	El Presidente	34		Hot Buttered Rum	8
Canadian	66	Emerson Martini	110		Hot Chocolate Almond	104
Canadian Cherry	66	English Cobbler	42		Hot Cider Cup	10
Canadian Summer	78	English Coffee	42		Hot Sangaree	118
Carol Channing	92	English Mule	42		Hot White Wine Punch	124
Casablanca	10	English Rose	12		Hurricane	62
Celebration	50					
Champagne Celebration	114	**F**			**I**	
Champagne Cocktail	124	Fallen Angel	10		Iced Coffee	98
Champagne Fizz	24	Ferrari	32		Irish Coffee	12
Champanska	124	Ferrari on the Rocks	98		Irish Eyes	124
Cheat's Eggnog	118	Fifty Fifty Vodka Martini	54		Irish Fix	30
Chelsea Hotel	64	Fireworks	106		Irish Martini	76
Cherry Daiquiri	112	Flirtini	100		Irish Rose	30
Cherry Flip	42	Floater	62		Isle of Skye	48
Cherry Rum Fizz	8	Fluffy Duck	54		Italian Lemonade	118
Cherry Sling	116	Flying Dutchman	54		Italian Martini	16
Chi Chi	14	Flying Scotsman	16			
Chicago	86	Foxtrot	80		**J**	
Chocatini	32	French Connection	32		Jack Frost	122
Chocoholic	22	French Rose	70		Jaded Lady	50
Chocolate Martini	10	French 75	88		Jamaican Coffee	46
Chocolate Orange	80	Fresh Lime & Ginger Soda	68		Jamaican Fizz	58
Christmas Cheer	120	Frisco Sour	22		Japanese Slipper	118
Christmas Cracker	122	Frozen Margarita	112		John Collins	120
Christmas Pudding	122	Fuzzy Navel	70		Joker, The	36
Cinnamon Apple	94				Journalist	58
Citrus Martini	68	**G**				
Claret Lemonade	78	Genoa Cocktail	94		**K**	
Classic Raki	68	Gimlet	12		Kamikaze	84
Coconut Shake	106	Gin & It	30		Kentucky Cocktail	38
Coffee Freeze	72	Gin & Sin	97		Kentucky Mule	110
Cognac & Mint Frappe	64	Gin & Tonic	38		Kir	70
Cola Float	32	Gin Crusta	26		Kir Raspberry	72
Corkscrew	14	Gin Daisy	52		Kir Royale	80
Corpse Reviver	104	Gin Sour	62			
Cosmo Twist	46	Gin Swizzle	98		**L**	
Cosmopolitan	82	Gin Zoom	116		La Habana	120
Country Gentleman	62	Gingenstein	52		Lady Godiva	48
Cuba Libre	22	Ginger Martini	102		Lemon Cola Float	66
		Ginger Snowball	124		Lemon Drop	18
		Glühwein	120		Lemon Kentucky	76